Transcriptions • Lessons • Bios • Photos

25 GREAT TRUMPET SOLOS

Featuring Pop, Rock, Jazz, Blues, and Swing Trumpet Legends, including Herb Alpert, Louis Armstrong, Chris Botti, Miles Davis, Maynard Ferguson, Dizzie Gillespie, Al Hirt, Chuck Mangione, and Many More

**by Eric J. Morones
featuring Steve Reid**

To access audio visit:
www.halleonard.com/mylibrary

Enter Code
6624-2012-5099-1772

Al Hirt, Dizzy Gillespie © Pictorial Press Ltd / Alamy
Miles Davis courtesy of Photofest
Chris Botti © Igor Vidyashev / Alamy
Louis Armstrong courtesy of Library of Congress
Herb Alpert © Pictorial Press Ltd / Alamy

ISBN 978-1-4803-0893-0

7777 W. BLUEMOUND RD. P.O. BOX 13819 MILWAUKEE, WI 53213

Visit Hal Leonard Online at
www.halleonard.com

Preface

25 *Great Trumpet Solos* is a collection of some of the most renowned trumpet solos and melodies ever recorded. The songs themselves are classics: famous, recognizable, and heard almost everywhere in the world. For the person who has always wanted to learn those famous trumpet melodies ("licks"), it's all here!

These solos were chosen using various criteria: popularity, acquirable publishing rights, chart position, and familiarity. Some are short and easy; others require serious "chops." Extensive research was done to provide accurate information about the solos, instruments, recording, and players.

About the Audio

The accompanying audio attempts to sound like the original recordings. The time code shown at the start of each solo transcription indicates the point where the solo begins on the original recording. There are two versions of each solo: 1) trumpet solo with accompaniment; 2) accompaniment only. This allows you to hear how the solo sounds, then to play it yourself with the accompaniment track. Though our goal was to replicate all solos and performances, there's nothing like the real thing, so we encourage you to listen to the original recordings.

All music on the recordings is performed by:

Steve Reid	trumpet, cornet, piccolo trumpet
Eric J. Morones	saxophone, clarinet, keyboards
Jordan Siegel	piano
Lucky Diaz	guitar
Greg Swiller	bass
Adam Gust	drums

Produced by Eric J. Morones

Recorded at Stagg Street Studios, Van Nuys, California

Mixed by Thai Long Ly at Bell Sound, Hollywood, California

Thank you to Jeff Schroedl, Hal Leonard Corporation, Thomas Stevens, Sidney Lazar, Lew Soloff, Dick Dale, my wife April, Nathan and Ava, and to the wonderful musicians on this project. A special word of thanks goes to trumpet player extraordinaire Steve Reid for playing these solos. He stepped into the shoes of all these great soloists, a feat that only a few could attempt with success.

Contents

Bix Beiderbecke

The oldest song in this book, "Riverboat Shuffle" sounds as fresh and timeless as it did almost 90 years ago.

Leon Bismark "Bix" Beiderbecke was born on March 10, 1903 in Davenport, Iowa. He began playing piano by ear at age three, later learning the organ from his mother. He taught himself the cornet while listening to early recordings of the Original Dixieland Jazz Band, as well as learning jazz off the riverboats that docked into downtown Davenport. He was sent to military school in 1921, skipping school for music ventures to Chicago. In Chicago, he joined the Wolverine Orchestra in 1923. Bix spent time with the Frank Trumbauer Orchestra in 1926, later joining the famous Paul Whiteman Orchestra.

Known for his distinctive tone, Beiderbecke's genius cornet playing was famous on recordings like "Singin'

Bix Beiderbecke

Hoagy Carmichael

the Blues," "I'm Coming, Virginia," "Clarinet Marmalade," and "Riverboat Shuffle." Though he never learned to read music, Bix was known for writing famous solo piano pieces like "In a Mist," "Flashes," and "In the Dark."

A hard drinker all his life, Bix died of an alcohol seizure in Queens, New York on August 6, 1931. He was 28 years old. Today, we still marvel at his solos for their originality, their unique phrasing, and the original timbres he could call his own. The 1950 film *Young Man with a Horn,* starring Kirk Douglas, was based on a biographical novel of Bix.

How to Play It

Almost 90 years old, this recording and trumpet solo give meaning to the word "timeless." When Bix Beiderbecke and the Wolverines recorded "Riverboat Shuffle" in 1924, it was Hoagy Carmichael's first recorded song. Recorded again three years later, the 1927 version (the one used here) with Frankie Trumbauer & His Orchestra was much faster, more defined, and featured a flashy melodic solo by Bix.

Bix Beiderbecke (center) with the Wolverines.

Bix comes out firing with his two-bar break, robust and confident. Notice his use of chord tones throughout the whole solo, which was the style of playing back then. His eighth notes are played with a quasi-swung, legato articulation, rather than a bona fide "swing jazz" articulation. (I'm not saying it doesn't swing, because it does!) His four-bar phrases contain textbook melodies. Notice the use of a wide vibrato on all the half notes. Measure 24 has some altered notes on the B♭7 chord; the ♭5, ♯9, ♮9, landing on the ♯11 for tension, then resolving to the tonic note of measure 25. Observe how Bix starts many of his solo lines on beat 2 from measures 3–19, using chromatically altered notes as well.

"One thing I like about jazz, kid, is that I don't know what's going to happen next. Do you?"

– Bix Beiderbecke

Vital Stats

Trumpet player: Bix Beiderbecke

Song: "Riverboat Shuffle"

Album: 10-inch 78-rpm recording

Age at time of recording: 21

Trumpet: Victor Cornet

Mouthpiece: Bach No. 7

Louis Armstrong

On June 28, 1928, 26-year-old Louis Armstrong walked into a studio in Chicago and recorded a performance, less than four minutes in duration, which would change the course of jazz history.

Louis Armstrong was born on August 4, 1901 in New Orleans, Louisiana. He started playing cornet at age 11 while he was in reform school. His idol, Joe "King" Oliver, became one of his first teachers and mentors. From 1919 to 1922 he played with various bands in dive bars from New Orleans to St. Louis. In 1922, Oliver himself took the teenaged Armstrong under his wing,

teaching him to play by ear. Taking him to Chicago, he fulfilled Armstrong's lifelong dream. Armstrong left Oliver's band in 1925 for a three-year stint in New York, where his amazing playing became the talk of the jazz community. He continued to perform with various groups, playing on Bessie Smith's classic 1925 recording of "St. Louis Blues."

Growing impatient to explore his own musical ideas, Armstrong formed a studio band that recorded as either the Hot Five or the Hot Seven, depending on its size. Louis Armstrong and the Hot Five or Hot Seven were soon considered one

of the greatest jazz groups in history, recording famous songs like "Heebie Jeebies" (possibly the first recording to feature scat singing), "Basin Street

Blues," "Muskrat Ramble," and "West End Blues." Armstrong's playing established a new standard for rhythmic and melodic complexity, technical mastery, sheer beauty, and emotional content. It was this revolutionary style and virtuosic technique that made him an international sensation. As a unique vocalist, he was known for his husky singing voice, scoring many popular hits like "A Kiss to Build a Dream On," "What a Wonderful World," and "Hello, Dolly." (See page 33.)

Known as "Satchmo" or "Pops," Armstrong died of a heart attack in his sleep on July 6, 1971, less than a month before his 70th birthday.

How to Play It

"West End Blues" is one of the most famous blues recordings ever, inducted into the Grammy Hall of Fame in 1974. Written by Joe "King" Oliver, the "West End" refers to the western-most point of Lake Pontchartrain in Orleans Parish, Louisiana. It's a standard 12-bar blues, most commonly performed as an instrumental, with lyrics added by Clarence Williams. King Oliver and His Dixie Syncopaters made the first recording of it on June 11, 1928, with Armstrong recording his classic version just weeks later. Playing cornet as well as scat singing, he is backed by a band that includes pianist Earl Hines. The song features two separate Armstrong solos.

Joe "King" Oliver

Solo 1

The genius of Armstrong's playing is evident in his unaccompanied beginning cadenza, one of the most influential and hard-to-copy solos in jazz history. Right out of the gate, his fiery tone and articulation hit you in the face. The opening three measures are like a trumpet fanfare, articulated over an implied D minor chord. They become almost a technical etude, showing Satchmo's flexibility and dexterity throughout the horn. Measures 4–7 display virtuoso chops in a double-time manner, creating Coltrane-like "sheets of sound."

Measure 8 is the melody, played with his trademark vibrato, wide and quick, on notes longer than an eighth note. Measures 16–19 show brilliant use of time and rhythm, with various laidback measures throughout. Measure 19 has a lip trill on beats 3–4.

Solo 2

Revisiting the melody, Armstrong this time starts an octave higher. With a long sustained high C, he adds vibrato with a big crescendo. Make sure you take a big breath, sustain, and pray! Measures 5–6 show his control of the horn and time, as he rushes the 16th-note blues lick at first, then plays it in time. After a brief piano solo, measures 12–14 are played with a controlled *ritardando*.

Interesting fact: Technology in 1928 didn't allow for immediate playback in the recording studio, so when Armstrong and his Hot Five ended their session, they had no idea how the record sounded. When Armstrong finally heard the recording weeks later, he was blown away.

Note: Lip trills in this solo and throughout the book are articulated by playing the note, then shaking the horn against your embouchure (or chops) like an aggressive or overdone vibrato.

"Sometimes the record would make me so sad, I'd cry up a storm. Other times, the same damn record would make me so happy."

–Billie Holiday
  on "West End Blues"

Vital Stats

Trumpet player: Louis Armstrong

Song: "West End Blues"

Album: 10-inch 78-rpm recording

Age at time of recording: 26

Trumpet: Buescher 10-22R

Mouthpiece: unknown

Joe "King" Oliver's Creole Jazz Band

Raymond Scott

Raymond Scott, composer of "The Toy Trumpet," was also an electronic music pioneer, inventor, and influential composer. Who knew he'd have such a huge influence on cartoon music for years to come?

Raymond Scott was born Harry Warnow on September 10, 1908 in Brooklyn, New York. A child prodigy, he was inspired by his older brother, Mark. Warnow graduated from Juilliard in 1931, where he studied piano, theory, and composition. After Juilliard, one of his first gigs was as pianist for the CBS Radio House Band, conducted by his brother, who became a successful conductor and violinist in his own right. Deciding to change his name to avoid favoritism charges for working under his brother, he randomly chose Raymond Scott out of a phone book. In 1934 he wrote a hit song, "Christmas Night in Harlem," that was recorded by Louis Armstrong.

In December 1936, with members of the CBS Band, Scott debuted his six-man Raymond Scott Quintette, which initially featured jazz giant Bunny Berigan on

© Pictorial Press Ltd / Alamy

Raymond Scott

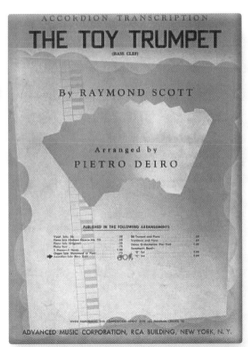

trumpet and drummer Johnny Williams, father of the well-known film composer John Williams. The Quintette – Scott's spelling – was actually a sextet, but its puckish leader quipped that calling the group by that title would take people's mind off the music. By early 1937, Scott's Quintette had become big stars on radio and records, landing a contract with 20th Century Fox to record for Hollywood films. The group's music sounded like cartoon compositions for a small group, with quirky hit songs like "Dinner Music for a Pack of Hungry Cannibals," "New Year's Eve in a Haunted House," "The Toy Trumpet," and "Powerhouse." Animation composer Carl Stalling used "Powerhouse"-derived melodies in dozens of Looney Tunes cartoons, including *Bugs Bunny, Daffy Duck,* and *Porky Pig.* Years later, "Powerhouse" was heard in *Duckman, The Ren and Stimpy Show,* and *The Simpsons,* among others.

Considered an engineer/electronic music pioneer, one time studying engineering at Brooklyn Technical High School, Scott invented and refined many electronic musical instruments from the 1950s through the 1970s. One of those instruments was the electronium, which was described as "an instantaneous composition and performance machine." He also invented the clavivox, which was a keyboard sound synthesizer and sequencer. It was later purchased by Berry Gordy of Motown. Scott eventually worked for Motown as their Director of Electronic Music Research and Development. Raymond Scott died at age 85 on February 8th, 1994.

Dave Wade was the trumpet player for the Raymond Scott Quintette. Sadly, no biographical information could be found.

How to Play It

On December 26, 1936, Scott's most famous composition, "The Toy Trumpet," debuted on the *Saturday Night Swing Session,* broadcast over CBS television. In 1938, Shirley Temple sang a vocal version of the song in the movie *Rebecca of Sunnybrook Farm,* while trumpeter Al Hirt had a hit with it in 1964.

Using a march-like articulation and phrasing, all the notes are played with a swing feel, using a straight mute throughout the solo. Notice how the flat thirds (B♭s) in the melody give the song a bluesy feel.

Measure 26 starts the B section of the song, played with a straight eighth-note feel. A classical trumpet approach is required, using no vibrato. Measures 64–71 cleverly quote "Taps." The E section, starting at measure 75, is played dirty and nasty, with lots of growls.

"There's a tremendous difference in performance if you skip the eyes."
–Raymond Scott

Vital Stats

Trumpet player: Dave Wade

Song: "The Toy Trumpet"

Album: 78-rpm recording

Age at time of recording: unknown

Trumpet: unknown

Mouthpiece: unknown

Photo by Metronome/Getty Images

Raymond Scott (seated at piano) plays with his Quintette

Bobby Hackett

Not only has "A String of Pearls" become a swing standard, so has the famous trumpet solo by Bobby Hackett.

Robert Leo "Bobby" Hackett was born on January 31, 1915 in Providence, Rhode Island. He played the ukulele at an early age and was, by 12, playing guitar and violin. He quit high school after his freshman year to play music full time. Known as "the New Bix," he performed in many local groups and by 1936 was leading his own bands. In 1937 he moved to New York, where he made his recording debut with the Dick Robertson Orchestra. Recording with Eddie Condon, he soon played with Benny Goodman, recording several songs at the historic Carnegie Hall Concert in 1938. Hackett signed with MCA Records to form and record his own band in 1939.

© ZUMA Press, Inc. / Alamy

Bobby Hackett

Between 1941–1942, he joined the Glenn Miller Orchestra on trumpet, eventually switching to guitar due to dental problems. (Because of ongoing challenges with his teeth, he played many gigs on guitar, even with Miller.)

After the Miller Orchestra, Bobby joined the music staff at NBC and ABC television. Actor Jackie Gleason, who formed a strong friendship with Hackett, produced a series of famous recordings featuring Hackett on trumpet.

Photo courtesy of http://www.kued.org

Glenn Miller Orchestra

These included *Music for Lovers Only* and *Music to Make You Misty*. Hackett became quite the studio musician, playing on many soundtracks, including the Fred Astaire musical comedy *Second Chorus* in 1940. He later played with the Casa Loma Orchestra and, from 1965–1967, was the official accompanist for Tony Bennett.

Bobby Hackett died of a heart attack on June 7, 1976 in Chatham, Massachusetts. He was 61 years old.

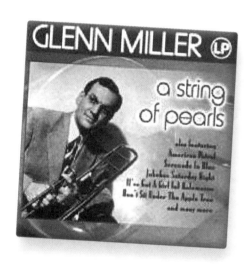

Glenn Miller was one of the most successful bandleaders in jazz. Born on March 1, 1904 in Clarinda, Iowa, he knew in high school that he wanted to be a musician. He first started on the mandolin, later switching to trombone. He attended the University of Colorado-Boulder for a brief period, but spent most of his time skipping classes for gigs. In search of the sound he heard in his head, he soon became a big band leader, arranger, and composer. He toured with several groups, writing many arrangements for different artists and co-writing "Room 1411" with Benny Goodman in 1928. Moving from Los Angeles to New York, he formed his own band in 1938, recording for RCA Victor.

Miller's breakout year came in 1939, with jukeboxes all around the country playing his tunes "Tuxedo Junction" and "Chattanooga Choo-Choo." Songs like "In the Mood," "Moonlight Serenade," "Pennsylvania 6-5000," and "A String of Pearls" became major hits of the Swing Era. In the early 1940s, he had 31 Top 10 hits (11 in 1941 alone).

On December 15, 1944, while flying over the English Channel, his plane suddenly disappeared. No one knows if his plane was shot down or if it crashed in the water uncontrollably. He was 40 years old.

Today, Miller's music is as popular as ever, still selling millions. "In the Mood" remains one of the most recognizable songs in popular music history.

How to Play It

"A String of Pearls" has become a Swing Era standard, along with Miller's "In the Mood" and "Pennsylvania 6-5000."

The Miller Orchestra recorded "A String of Pearls" in 1941. It was composed by Jerry Gray, with lyrics by Eddie DeLange. The record later hit No. 1 in the U.S. for two weeks on the *Billboard* Best Sellers chart.

The solo is played with swing-eighths. Notice how the piece is almost a technical etude, based on arpeggio patterns. Measures 1–2 feature triads in root position, while measures 5–6 are first-inversion triads, all played from the top down. Measure 9 uses triads in root position, starting with the tonic note. Check out the interval leap of a ninth in measure 11, on beat four.

Glenn Miller

"By giving the public a rich and full melody, distinctly arranged and well played, all the time creating new tone colors and patterns, I feel we have a better chance of being successful."

–Glenn Miller

Vital Stats

Trumpet player: Bobby Hackett

Song: "A String of Pearls"

Album: 78-rpm single

Age at time of recording: 26

Trumpet: French Besson Cornet

Mouthpiece: unknown

2:03

Moderate Swing (♩ = 131) (♫ = ♩♪)

Music by Jerry Gray

Dizzy Gillespie

With his unique balloon cheeks and broken angled trumpet, Dizzy Gillespie was a jazz pioneer, and one its most influential musicians.

John Birks "Dizzy" Gillespie was born on October 21, 1917 in Cheraw, South Carolina. His father was a local bandleader, so instruments were always available for him to play. He started on the piano at four, later beginning the trombone, then switching to trumpet at age 12. Hearing his idol Roy Eldridge inspired him to become a jazz musician.

Following high school, Gillespie studied at the Laurinburg Institute in North Carolina on a music scholarship. He later gigged around Philadelphia, then moved to New York in 1937, playing with Teddy Hill, Cab Calloway, Earl Hines, and Billy Eckstine. He started writing music for Woody Herman and Jimmy Dorsey, quickly earning his nickname "Dizzy" due to his unpredictable and crazy behavior. In 1953, a fellow musician accidentally sat on his trumpet, bending the bell into an irregular shape. Dizzy, liking the way it sounded, left it. This bent trumpet became one of his famous

Dizzy Gillespie

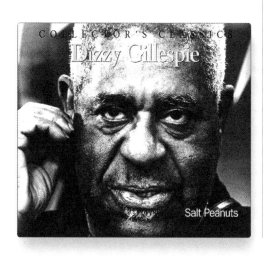

Salt Peanuts

trademarks, but it was his fiery playing and recordings with the great Charlie Parker that soon revolutionized music with "bebop."

In bebop, Dizzy set new standards on the trumpet with his high note wails, rhythmic shifts, and advanced harmonic playing. As a composer, he wrote many jazz standards, like "A Night in Tunisia," "Groovin' High," "Hot House," and "Salt Peanuts." He was also a key leader in bringing Afro-Cuban/Latin music to prominence, revolutionizing rhythms of Afro-Cuban, Caribbean, and Brazilian music with his Latin band featuring Chano Pozo.

As leader of the United Nations Orchestra, Dizzy become a music ambassador for the United States, traveling the world with his unique playing and arrangements. He was inducted into *Down Beat* magazine's Jazz Hall of Fame in 1960, and won a Grammy Award for Best Jazz Performance by a Soloist in 1976. In 1990, he was honored with the Grammy Lifetime Achievement Award. Throughout his remaining years, he kept busy, touring relentlessly and mentoring musicians from around the world.

Gillespie died of pancreatic cancer on January 6, 1993 in Englewood, New Jersey. He was 75 years old.

How to Play It

Gillespie and drummer Kenny Clarke wrote "Salt Peanuts." Dizzy Gillespie & His All-Stars recorded it on May 11, 1945. While the chanted phrase "Salt peanuts, salt peanuts!" is closely identified with Gillespie, the musical motif upon which it is based predates Gillespie/Clarke: It appeared as a repeated six-note instrumental phrase played on piano by Count Basie on his July 2, 1941 recording of "Basie Boogie."

Serious high-note chops are needed to play this, as well as fast chops. Make sure you practice the solo slowly, using a metronome. Measure 22 seems to quote and turn "Honeysuckle Rose" into a bebop lick, with a leap of a major sixth in measure 23. The use of eighth-note lines throughout the solo is common language in bebop, incorporating lots of passing tones, chromatics, use of chord extensions/structures (starting on the ninth, 11th, 13th of the chord), all at a fast tempo.

Interesting note: There's a five-bar solo break, instead of the standard four, before the band enters at measure 6 of the form.

I don't know how they did this, but every member of the rhythm section comes in correctly on the right bar of the form!

> *"I don't recall how the tune got that name "Salt Peanuts," but as a tune on its own, it became more elaborate than just a riff."*
>
> –Dizzy Gillespie

Vital Stats

Trumpet player: Dizzy Gillespie

Song: "Salt Peanuts"

Album: 78-rpm record

Age at time of recording: 27

Trumpet: Martin Committee

Mouthpiece: unknown

Dizzie Gillespie Big Band

By John "Dizzy" Gillespie and Kenny Clarke
Copyright © 1943 UNIVERSAL MUSIC CORP.
Copyright Renewed
All Rights Reserved   Used by Permission

Clifford Brown

"Cherokee (Indian Love Song)" is the jazz tune used to test one's skills and abilities on the horn, usually at a ridiculously fast tempo. We can thank Clifford Brown for setting the bar high on that one!

Clifford "Brownie" Brown was born on October 30, 1930 in Wilmington, Delaware. Coming from a gifted family, Brownie inherited his interest in music from his father, who had many instruments around the house. He received his first trumpet at age 15, studying classical and jazz in high school. Considered a math genius, Clifford studied music and mathematics at Delaware State College, later transferring to Maryland State College on a music scholarship. He played with J.J. Johnson and Ernie Henry around Philadelphia early in his career, and considered Fats Navarro his early main influence.

At age 19, due to another trumpet player being late, Brownie sat in with Dizzy Gillespie and started making a buzz as the next great trumpeter. In 1950, he was severely injured in a car accident that left him hospitalized for almost a year. Gillespie visited him during this time and encouraged him to get well and to continue to pursue music seriously. After his recovery, Clifford soon became an influential and highly rated trumpeter, known for his warm tone, impeccable sense of rhythm, crisp articulation, and amazing control over the instrument. He also played piano, drums, and vibes very well. He toured with R&B artist Chris Powell between 1952–53, also playing with Lionel Hampton, Lou Donaldson,

© Ross Burdick / CTSIMAGES

Clifford Brown

and Tadd Dameron. Clifford joined drummer Max Roach to form the classic Clifford Brown/Max Roach Quintet in March 1954. That same year, he won *Down Beat* magazine's critics' poll for the New Star of the Year.

Sadly, on June 26, 1956, Clifford was killed, along with pianist Richie Powell and Powell's wife Nancy, when their car skidded off the Pennsylvania Turnpike during a rainstorm. He left only four years' worth of landmark recordings, but his mark as a soloist and composer in that short time will last forever.

How to Play It

"Cherokee (Indian Love Song)" is a jazz standard written by Ray Noble, originally intended as the first of five movements for his *Indian Suite*. Although it was a hit for the Charlie Barnet Orchestra in 1939, "Cherokee" wasn't considered a vehicle for jazz improvisation until Charlie Parker recorded and raised eyebrows with it, most famously with his contrafact "Ko-Ko." It was Brown who raised eyebrows with the song the next time.

Fast technique is needed to play these two brilliant choruses of solo. Practice the solo away from the recording first, slowly and with a metronome. This solo can easily be considered an etude in itself. Notice the continuous use of eyebrow-raising eighth-note lines, utilizing the bebop language of passing tones, chromatics, and use of chord extensions/ structures. When playing, use proper jazz articulation on all the eighth notes.

"To me, the name of Clifford Brown will always remain synonymous with the very essence of musical and moral maturity."

–Quincy Jones

Vital Stats

Trumpet player: Clifford Brown

Song: "Cherokee (Indian Love Song)"

Album: *Study in Brown*

Age at time of recording: 24

Trumpet: Blessing Artist model

Mouthpiece: unknown

© Everett Collection Inc / Alamy

Ray Noble

Cherokee (Indian Love Song)

Pérez Prado

Pérez Prado made the mambo the dance craze of an era. His version of "Cherry Pink and Apple Blossom White" only confirmed him as the "King of the Mambo."

Dámaso Pérez was born on December 11, 1916 in Mantanzas, Cuba. He studied classical piano as a child, and by the time he finished high school he was playing organ and piano in cinemas and local clubs. In 1942, at age 26, he moved to Havana, Cuba where he played in various groups and did arrangements for many bands. It was around this time that Pérez's conception of the mambo – "an Afro-Cuban rhythm with a dash of American swing" – came into play. He left Cuba in 1947 and settled in Mexico City, where he formed his own ensemble. He became musical director for several Mexican films, as well as an occasional actor. Pérez signed with RCA Mexico in 1949, later signing with RCA Victor. The latter released his hit "Mambo No. 5" in 1950; it was sampled by Lou Bega for his 1999 song, "Mambo No. 5 (A Little Bit Of…)."

By the 1950s, the Mambo sensation was hitting Mexico and South America, where it soon traveled to the U.S. Pérez took advantage of this new popularity and decided to tour the States. He legally changed his name to Pérez Prado in 1955, by this time already known as the "King of Mambo." He scored a No. 1 hit with "Cherry Pink and Apple Blossom White" and with "Patricia" in 1958. With scorching brass charts and fiery percussion, the "Pérez Sound" had other famous hits, including "Mambo No. 8," "Mambo Jambo," and "Que Rico El Mambo."

Over the years, as the Mambo craze died, Prado returned to Mexico permanently, where he remained a huge star. He died of a stroke on September 14, 1989 in Mexico City.

Billy Regis was the solo trumpeter on "Cherry Pink and Apple Blossom White." Unfortunately, no biographical information could be found.

© Pictorial Press Ltd / Alamy

Pérez Prado

How to Play It

Louis Guglielmi, a Spanish composer of Italian extraction who wrote under the pseudonym Louisguy, penned the melody for Edith Piaf's lyrics "La vie en rose." He wrote "Cherry Pink and Apple Blossom White" ("Cerisier rose et pommier blanc" in French, "Cereza rosa" in Spanish) in 1950. It has French lyrics, but mostly is famous for its instrumental versions. Prado's "Cha Cha" version of the song spent 10 weeks at No. 1, and a total of 26 weeks on the *Billboard* charts. The song was also featured in the 1955 movie *Underwater!*, starring Jane Russell. (Pérez Prado himself made a cameo appearance.)

The song is basically just the melody with no solo sections. Be sure to use a shaky vibrato throughout. To play that famous "Cherry Pink" note on the opening melody, half-valve the note, and bend the pitch downward with your embouchure. Letter B (measure 10) is played by the saxes, but is included here for you to play along. Pay close attention to all notated articulations. Measure 30 has the melody played as is the first time, then up an octave on the repeat. Try your best to play those high notes, and don't hurt yourself on the 16th-note run (up an octave) into measure 35, landing on the high F.

"I am a collector of cries and noises, elemental ones like seagulls on the shore, winds through the trees, men at work in a foundry. Mambo is a movement back to nature, by means of rhythms based on such cries and noises, and on simple joys."

–Pérez Prado

Vital Stats

Trumpet player: Billy Regis

Song: "Cherry Pink and Apple Blossom White"

Album: *Mambo Mania*

Age at time of recording: unknown

Trumpet: unknown

Mouthpiece: unknown

Miles Davis

Miles Davis, one of the geniuses of jazz, is responsible for one of the most famous and definitive jazz records of all time.

Miles Dewey Davis III was born on May 16, 1926 in Alton, Illinois. His father, a respected dentist, gave him a trumpet at age 13. By 16, he was playing professionally, taking lessons with Joseph Gustat, principal trumpet in the St. Louis Symphony Orchestra. Davis's early gigs included playing with Clark Terry, Dizzy Gillespie, and Billy Eckstine. He studied music at Juilliard, but his real motivation for going to New York was to find his hero, Charlie Parker. He eventually got that chance, later replacing Dizzy Gillespie and recording with Parker.

Miles made his first solo recordings as a bandleader in 1946. Around 1948, he befriended Canadian composer and arranger Gil Evans. Together, they recorded some of greatest albums in jazz: *Birth of the Cool, Miles Ahead,* and later, *Sketches of Spain.* Davis made music history and an indelible impact with his famous jazz quintets and sextets that featured members like John Coltrane, Cannonball Adderly, Wayne Shorter, and Herbie Hancock. The classic ensemble on 1959's *Kind of Blue* album included pianist Bill Evans, Coltrane, Adderly, Jimmy Cobb, and Paul Chambers. It has been regarded by many critics as the greatest jazz album of all time, becoming Davis's *magnum opus.*

Known as a music innovator, Miles took another direction with his "electric" period. Albums like *Miles in the Sky, Bitches Brew, In a Silent Way,* and *On the*

Miles Davis

Corner not only invented jazz fusion, but also had a huge impact on many rock and roll musicians and albums. In the 1980s, after a long hiatus, Miles returned to experiment with music once again. This time he went in a pop direction, creating classic interpretations of songs such as Michael Jackson's "Human Nature" and Cyndi Lauper's "Time After Time." Across his career, Miles garnered 14 Grammy Awards, including the Lifetime Achievement Award in 1990.

Miles Davis died from the combined effects of pneumonia, respiratory failure, and a stroke on September 28, 1991. He was posthumously inducted into the Rock and Roll Hall of Fame in 2006.

As one of the greatest musical visionaries of all time, Davis's music and playing will continue to live on and inspire.

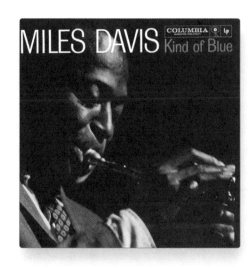

"Don't play what's there. Play what's not there."

–Miles Davis

Vital Stats

Trumpet player: Miles Davis

Song: "So What"

Album: *Kind of Blue*

Age at time of recording: 33

Trumpet: Martin Committee

Mouthpiece: Heim

How to Play It

Released on August 17, 1959, the album *Kind of Blue* is a masterpiece. It was rated No. 12 on *Rolling Stone* magazine's 500 Greatest Albums of All Time in 2003. With no rehearsals or chord changes – only scales to improvise on – this was jazz at its purest.

"So What," the opening track, is a modal tune consisting of only two chord changes throughout the song's AABA form. It is quite different from other jazz tunes that incorporate many complex, fast harmonic changes. The piano intro was written by Gil Evans, based on a 1910 piano piece ("Voiles") by French composer Claude Debussy. Davis's solo is laid back, using a lyrical, melodic style throughout, so be sure to "lay back" on the solo.

© AF archive / Alamy

Bill Evans

So What

Dick Dale

When those rocking, opening licks of "Misirlou" started off the movie *Pulp Fiction,* you just knew you were on a different wave!

Guitarist Dick Dale was born Richard Anthony Monsour on May 14, 1937 in Boston, Massachusetts. He moved to Orange County, California in his teen years, where he learned to surf – and became interested in music. His uncle, an oud player, became his first musical influence. Dale first played trumpet in high school, with Harry James as his idol. Later, he taught himself the ukulele, drums, and guitar. Since he never took music lessons, he never learned how to read or write music.

Searching for the sound he heard in his head while he surfed, Dale began experimenting with various tones on his guitars. He befriended guitar inventor Leo Fender, who gave Dale his new invention to play with: the Fender Stratocaster electric guitar. Wishing to achieve on the electric guitar what Gene Krupa had achieved on drums, Dale became known for blowing out amps in search of that elusive sound. Due to these mishaps, Dale became involved in the invention of the first 100-watt guitar amplifier. (*Guitar Player* magazine later called him the Father of Heavy Metal.) Dale was also a pioneer of electronic reverb, an idea he got from trying to copy the Hammond organ sound. What became known as the "wet" sound would soon be considered the "surf" sound, making Dale the "King of Surf Guitar."

Photofest

Dick Dale

In 1961, Dale recorded his first song, "Let's Go Trippin'," on his debut album *Surfer's Choice*. This album also included the famous American surf song "Misirlou." The Beach Boys recorded their own version of the song on the 1963 album *Surfin' USA*. It has also been covered by bands like the Surfaris and the Trashmen.

After some health issues in the 1970s, Dale retired from music, but returned in the 1980s. He received a Grammy Award nomination for his music in the 1987 movie *Back to the Beach*, and made a cameo appearance in the film. He regained major popularity again in 1994 when "Misirlou" was used in the hit movie *Pulp Fiction*. Since then it's been used in many movies and commercials, and even sampled by the Black Eyed Peas for their song "Pump It" in 2006.

Dale was inducted into the Nashville Musicians Hall of Fame in 2009. Since playing country music was always his first love, it was a great honor for him to be inducted. A cancer survivor, Dale is still traveling and touring at age 75. According to Dale himself, "When I die, it's not going to be in a wheel chair, but onstage with one explosion of body parts!"

How to Play It

"Misirlou" is a famous song for guitarists, but the trumpet solo is just as memorable. It is a popular Greek song that dates back to 1927. (The word "misirlou" translates as "Egyptian girl.") Michalis Patrinos recorded a version in 1930, and in 1941 Nicholas Roubanis released a jazz instrumental arrangement, crediting himself as the composer. Dale created a new version of the song after a kid asked him to write a tune that used only one string. With his unique *staccato* picking style – which he had developed by copying Gene Krupa's drumming – it was a perfect match.

The melody is based on a Hijaz Kar Scale or double harmonic scale (F♯-G-B-C-C♯-D-F). Dale's friend Tommy Stewart played the trumpet solo because Dale couldn't play guitar and trumpet at the same time. (Remember, this was before multi-track recording was invented.) In later years, Dale himself played the trumpet solo during performances.

The trumpet solo, unlike the famous guitar part, is technically simple. Play with a loud sound and a very shaky vibrato, the more overblown and obnoxious the better! Notice how the first eight measures stay on the chord tones. Measure 9 to the end features Mariachi-style turns, with measure 14 using the scale from the melody, with a growling sound.

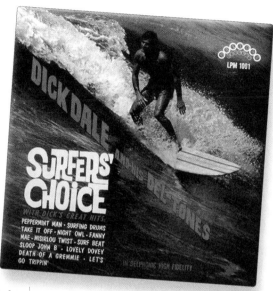

> *"When I play, it's like I'm fighting you."*
>
> –Dick Dale

Vital Stats

Trumpet player: Tommy Stewart

Song: "Misirlou"

Album: *Surfer's Choice*

Age at time of recording: unknown

Trumpet: unknown

Mouthpiece: unknown

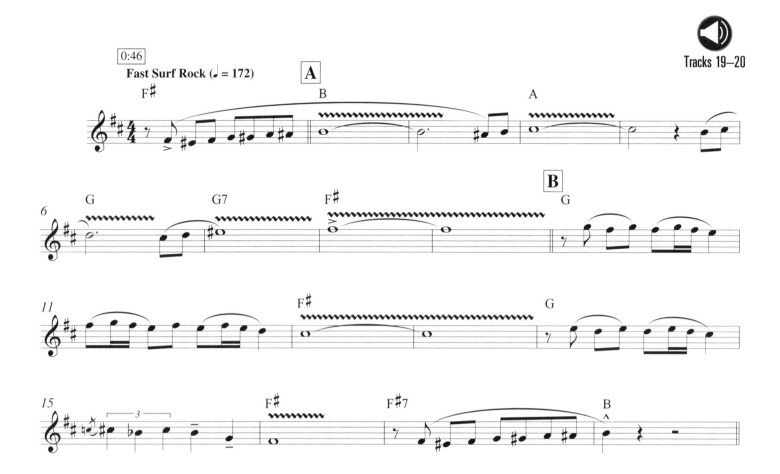

Louis Armstrong

Leave it to trumpet virtuoso Louis Armstrong to have two masterpiece solos in this book!

(For Louis Armstrong's biographical information, see page 4.)

How to Play It

"Hello, Dolly!" is the title song from the 1964 Tony Award-winning musical of the same name, featuring Carol Channing. It was written by music theater composer and lyricist Jerry Herman. Louis Armstrong's 1963 version sold millions and received two Grammy Awards in 1965 – for Best Vocal Performance and for Song of the Year. Satchmo's recording knocked the Beatles' "Can't Buy Me Love" off the No. 1 spot in the U.S. In 1969, Armstrong recorded a new version with Barbra Streisand for the movie *Hello, Dolly!* It has since become a pop standard recorded by many artists, and was inducted into the Grammy Hall of Fame in 2001.

Louis Armstrong

Armstrong's classic version features both his trademark voice and a simple, great solo. Staying close to the melody, he adds a number of beautiful embellishments. Make sure you use an open plunger, pay attention to all the articulations throughout, and perform note shakes on half notes and dotted-quarter notes. Lay back on the time in measure 7.

Jerry Herman

Beginning at measure 18, Armstrong shows what he can do, playing simple melodies to absolute perfection. Starting on measure 25, he returns back to the melody before letting the trombone take over until the end.

"Musicians don't retire. They stop when there's no more music in them."

–Louis Armstrong

Vital Stats

Trumpet player: Louis Armstrong

Song: "Hello, Dolly!"

Album: 45-rpm single

Age at time of recording: 62

Trumpet: unknown

Mouthpiece: unknown

Al Hirt

Al Hirt's "Java" is a happy, infectious song that, once you hear it, you can't get it out of your head!

Alois Maxwell Hirt was born on November 7, 1922 in New Orleans, Louisiana. He started playing the trumpet at age six and was playing professionally at age 16. (An early gig, during his high school years, was sounding post time at a local horse track.) In 1940, he studied classical trumpet at the Cincinnati Conservatory of Music and during World War II was a bugler in the U.S. Army. After the army, he went on to play with the Dorsey Brothers, Benny Goodman, and Horace Heidt's Orchestra. In the mid 1950s, Hirt recorded and played with his friend, New Orleans clarinetist Pete Fountain. He formed a group called the Dixieland Six that played in Las Vegas. While in Vegas, he was spotted and hired by Dinah Shore for her TV variety show.

Hirt signed with RCA Victor in 1960, which was the beginning of a decade of huge success. He scored several Top 10 albums, such as *Honey in the Horn* and *Cotton Candy*. These included big hits like "Java," "Cotton Candy," and "Sugar Lips." The latter became the theme song for the game show *Eye Guess* in 1964. That year saw the release of the best-selling album *"Pops" Goes the Trumpet,* recorded with Arthur Fiedler and the Boston Pops. This LP featured "The Toy Trumpet" (see page 8), making the song as popular as ever. *Billboard* named him Top Instrumentalist in 1965. In 1966, Hirt played the theme for TV's *The Green Hornet,* a jazz-style arrangement of Rimsky-Korsakov's "Flight of the Bumblebee" by Billy May. Other notable

Al Hirt

performances for Hirt included playing at John F. Kennedy's inauguration (1961) and headlining the half-time show of Super Bowl I (1967).

In the late 1960s, Hirt opened his own jazz club in the French Quarter of New Orleans. It remained open until 1983.

Hirt died of liver failure on April 27, 1999 in New Orleans. He was 76 years old. With more than 50 albums, four gold records, and one platinum, it's obvious Hirt's masterful playing and songs will remain timeless.

How to Play It

Al Hirt, who was nicknamed the Round Mound of Sound, had his biggest hit with "Java," which sold over a million copies. The song first appeared on the 1958 LP

The Wild Sounds of New Orleans by New Orleans producer/songwriter/pianist Allen Toussaint. Hirt's version was the first single from his best-selling album, *Honey in the Horn,* becoming his first and biggest hit on the U.S. pop charts. In 1964, it reached No. 4 on the *Billboard* Hot 100, spending four weeks at No. 1 on the easy listening charts. It also won the Grammy Award for Best Performance by an Orchestra or Instrumentalist later that year.

Just under two minutes in length, the song is catchy and simple! Make sure you play the whole solo straight, in an almost comical way. The first half of the solo (sections A B C D) is basically the melody. Section E is an eight-bar solo that showcases Hirt's control and flexibility.

> *"I'm a pop commercial musician and I've got a successful format."*
> –Al Hirt

Vital Stats

Trumpet player: Al Hirt

Song: "Java"

Album: *Honey in the Horn*

Age at time of recording: 42

Trumpet: LaBlanc Signature Model made by Courtois

Mouthpiece: Jet-Tone Al Hirt Model

Carl Lender

Allen Toussaint

David Mason

David Mason may be the most-heard trumpet player in rock and roll history. Little did he know that a session for a band he'd never heard of would make him famous.

Mason was born on April 2, 1926 in London, England. He studied with Ernest Hall at the Royal College of Music. After training there, he became a member of the Royal Opera House Orchestra, later becoming principal trumpet for the Royal Philharmonic Orchestra. In 1958, he was the flugelhorn soloist for the world premiere performance of Ralph Vaughan Williams's Symphony No. 9.

Mason's featured performance in Bach's Brandenburg Concerto No. 2 on British television caught the eye and ear of Beatles member Paul McCartney. McCartney was searching for that "special something" for his new song "Penny Lane" and immediately felt Mason could provide it. Mason was soon called to the famed Abbey Road Studios by Beatles producer George Martin, who asked him to record an eight-bar solo for the song. Not only did he make the track, but ended up playing on other Beatles songs such as

David Mason

"A Day in the Life," "Magical Mystery Tour," and "All You Need Is Love."

From 1970 to 1998, Mason was professor of trumpet at the Royal College of Music in London. He died of leukemia at age 85 on April 29, 2011.

Perhaps the greatest group of all time, the Beatles are the best-selling band in history. Formed in Liverpool, England (with members Paul McCartney, John Lennon, George Harrison, and Ringo Starr), their records have sold more than a billion copies. Their influence on rock and roll music and its musicians and songwriters cannot be overestimated.

In the early days, the band called themselves the Quarrymen, later changing their name to the Beatles. They signed with EMI's Parlophone Records in 1962, releasing their first single, "Love Me Do," off their debut LP *Please Please Me*. After their famous performance on the *Ed Sullivan Show* in 1964, the band's music and popularity took off like a rocket. With hit singles like "She Loves You," "Can't Buy Me Love," "Yesterday," "Penny Lane," "Let It Be," and many others, and best-selling albums such as *Sgt. Pepper's Lonely Hearts Club Band*, *Revolver*, and *Abbey Road*, they can easily be considered the world's most famous rock group.

A view down Penny Lane

They won seven Grammy Awards and charted 45 gold albums, six diamond albums, and 39 platinum albums in the U.S. alone. They hold the No. 1 spot on *Billboard* magazine's list of all-time successful artists.

How to Play It

"Penny Lane" was originally intended to be on the landmark Beatles album *Sgt. Pepper's Lonely Hearts Club Band.* Yet, it was eventually used as a double A-side single with "Strawberry Fields Forever." Both songs were later included on the U.S. *Magical Mystery Tour* album in November 1967. McCartney had originally planned to use another instrument for the middle solo, but was impressed with the sound of the piccolo trumpet he heard on TV. Mason was called into the session and McCartney apparently lined out the solo on the piano, showing him what notes to play. After auditioning nine different trumpets, it was agreed that the piccolo trumpet sounded best.

The B♭ piccolo trumpet is pitched an octave higher than the standard B♭ trumpet. If you play the "Penny Lane" solo on a normal B♭ trumpet, reading the music "as is" will sound one octave lower than the famous recording. If you don't own a piccolo, try playing the solo up an octave. (Just don't hurt yourself!) The solo appears harder than it really is, with those scary-looking 32nd notes, triplets, and the key of C♯. The good news is that all the lines pretty much move diatonically up the scale.

Use the downbeats as your target notes, and play with a classical trumpet style.

Photofest

The Beatles

"I did not even know who the Beatles were."

–David Mason

Bb Piccolo Tpt.   1:08

Hugh Masekela

Hugh Masekela became a household name with his version of "Grazing in the Grass."

Hugh Ramopolo Masekela was born on April 4, 1939 in Kwa-Guqa Township, Witbank, South Africa. He began singing and playing piano at age six, and took up the trumpet at age 14 after seeing the film *Young Man with a Horn,* based on the life of Bix Beiderbecke. Archbishop Trevor Huddleston gave him his first trumpet from St. Peter's Secondary School, an instrument previously owned by Louis Armstrong. He became influenced by the street, church, and work songs he heard in his neighborhood as a child. In 1959, he formed the Jazz Epistles, the first South African jazz band ever to make recordings.

Aided by musical luminaries Yehudi Menuhin and John Dankworth, he left apartheid, South Africa in 1960 to attend London's Guildhall School of Music. Around that time, Hugh visited the United States and decided to study classical trumpet at the Manhattan School of Music. He was there from 1960 to 1964.

Masekela had a hit with the song "Up, Up and Away" in 1968, but it was a year later that he reached the top of the charts with the No. 1 song "Grazing in the Grass," selling over four million copies. He went on to record with many jazz artists, as well as pop artists like the Byrds and Paul Simon, with whom he toured in the 1980s. Many of his songs were an inspiration in the fight against apartheid in South Africa, where his song "Bring Him Back Home" became the anthem for activist Nelson Mandela's release from prison in 1990.

Over the last 50 years, Masekela has released more than 40 albums. Today, he still tours and records and is involved with a musical theater he founded in South Africa.

Hugh Masekela

Hugh Masekela

How to Play It

"Grazing in the Grass" was composed by Philemon Hou. Masekela's million-selling, No. 1 hit version was nominated for a Grammy Award for Best Contemporary Pop Performance–Instrumental in 1968. It was inspired by an earlier recording of his called "Mr. Bull No. 5." The group Friends of Distraction recorded a vocal version of it in 1969; it became a hit at No. 5 on the *Billboard* charts. Today, it's as popular as ever, still recorded by many artists – recently by smooth jazz musicians Boney James and Rick Braun – and is heard in many movies.

Section A is the song's melody, featuring the tenor sax in unison (breaking away to harmony at times). Be sure to play all the notated articulations. Section B is Masekela's solo, using lots of pulsating 16th notes throughout. Measures 13–16 are a repeated call-and-response line, with measures 18–20 featuring some bluesy trumpet playing. Measure 21 begins a 16th-note phrase that uses half valves (1 + 3) all the way up to measure 26. This section shows that playing just one note with inflection and attitude can make a solo sing and groove! No bebop here, just some funky playing by Masekela.

"Before Louis Armstrong, the world was definitely square, just like Christopher Columbus thought."

–Hugh Masekela

Vital Stats

Trumpet player: Hugh Masekela

Song: "Grazing in the Grass"

Album: *The Promise of a Future*

Age at time of recording: 28

Trumpet: unknown

Mouthpiece: unknown

Words by Harry Elston
Music by Philemon Hou
© 1968 (Renewed) CHERIO CORP.
All Rights Reserved

Lew Soloff

"Spinning Wheel" is a unique composition. The fact that it was both a pop hit and featured an amazing jazz trumpet solo make it even more unusual.

Lew Soloff was born on February 20, 1944 in Brooklyn, New York. Raised in Lakewood, New Jersey, he studied piano at an early age, taking up the trumpet when he was ten years old. His interest in the instrument grew steadily, thanks to the record collections of his uncle and grandfather. Lew entered the Eastman School of Music in 1961, eventually doing a year of graduate school at Juilliard. His primary influence was Miles Davis. When he settled in New York, he played with the famous Latin jazz musician Machito, which gave Soloff a reputation in the Latin jazz community. He also attended jam sessions with Phil Woods, Pepper Adams, Elvin Jones, and Duke Pearson. In 1966, he played with Maynard Ferguson, the Joe Henderson/Kenny Dorham Big Band, and joined the Gil Evans Group. Evans became his musical godfather, with a creative relationship that lasted to Evans's death in 1988.

Soloff's work with the jazz/rock band Blood, Sweat & Tears made him a rock

Lew Soloff

star. He played with the band from 1968 to 1973 and racked up nine gold records and a Grammy. After Blood, Sweat & Tears, he played with everyone from Miles Davis to Barbra Streisand. He was the lead trumpeter for the Carnegie Hall Big Band and has released more than seven solo recordings. As a studio musician, he's played on films that include *The Big Lebowski, The Mambo King,* and *The Color of Money.*

Today, Lew is as active as ever, doing studio sessions, giving clinics at universities, playing with Carla Bley's Big Band, the Manhattan Jazz Quintet, and leading his own Lew Soloff Quartet. He's been on faculty at the Manhattan School of Music for the past 20 years, and is an adjunct faculty member at the New School.

Blood, Sweat & Tears have left a huge mark on rock and jazz since 1968. With a stellar horn section as famous as that of the band Chicago, its players have included a who's who of famous jazz

and rock musicians. Formed in 1967 by guitarist and singer Al Kooper, they fused all styles – from classical, rock, and jazz – into their music, releasing their first album, *Child Is Father to the Man,* in 1968. The follow-up self-titled *Blood, Sweat & Tears* album rocketed them to huge success. With new lead singer David Clayton-Thomas in the band, the album won five Grammy Awards, beating out the Beatles' *Abbey Road* for Album of the Year, and selling over four million copies. Hit singles like "Spinning Wheel," "And When I Die," and "You've Made Me So Very Happy" led them to headliner status at Woodstock in 1969. They scored another hit with a cover of Carole King's "Hi-De-Ho" on *Blood, Sweat & Tears 3* (1970). After being dropped by Columbia Records in 1976, Clayton-Thomas left to be a solo artist, with the band going through dozens of personnel changes in the years that followed.

Today, the band is still touring, minus any of the original members.

How to Play It

"Spinning Wheel" was Blood, Sweat & Tears' biggest hit, selling over three million copies. Written by lead singer David Clayton-Thomas and arranged by the band's saxophonist Fred Lipsius, it peaked at No. 2 on the *Billboard* Hot 100 and was nominated for three Grammys, winning one for Best Instrumental Arrangement. For the released single version, the trumpet solo was removed, although the version heard nowadays is the one from the album, with trumpet solo.

Soloff's solo is bebop oriented, played in the trumpet's high range. Notice how the first three measures quote the song's melody, at the request of Clayton-Thomas. Measures 17–20 outline the F♯7 chord with legato articulation, with measures 21–24 going right back to swinging eighth notes.

Be sure to swing all the eighth notes, and use lots of air support for the high note lines.

"This was the second take of the solo; the first take was my favorite! David [Clayton-Thomas] suggested on the second take I start off the solo quoting the melody, so I did."

–Lew Soloff

Photo by Hulton Archive/Getty Images

Blood, Sweat & Tears

Vital Stats

Trumpet player: Lew Soloff

Song: "Spinning Wheel"

Album: *Blood, Sweat & Tears*

Age at time of recording: 23

Trumpet: Mt. Vernon Bach (22,000 series)

Mouthpiece: Mt. Vernon Bach 5C

Lee Loughnane

The band Chicago is famous not only for making pop hits, but for featuring one of the greatest horn sections of all time!

Lee Loughnane (pronounced LOCK-nane) was born on October 21, 1946 in Elwood Park, Illinois. He was encouraged in his musical pursuits by his father, who played trumpet. Lee enjoyed playing along with his dad's collection of big band records, and his early influences were Maynard Ferguson, Clifford Brown, Doc Severinsen, and Marvin Stamm. He studied trumpet with John Nuzzo before attending DePaul University in Chicago. At DePaul, Lee and five other musicians formed a Top 40 cover band called the Big Thing. This group of musicians would soon become rock superstars. The band moved to Los Angeles, where they changed their name to the Chicago Transit Authority, later shortening it to Chicago, after the CTA threatened legal action. As a founding member of Chicago, Loughnane also has songwriting credits for tunes like "Call on Me," "No Tell Lover," and "Together Again."

Lee Loughnane

Today, Lee still plays trumpet with the band, having taken charge in the band's re-mastering of their music catalogue. He also has a star on the Hollywood Walk of Fame with his Chicago bandmates.

Chicago is one of the longest-running and most successful rock groups in history. They have sold over 38 million records, have 22 gold, 18 platinum, and 21 Top 10 singles. The band is second only to the Beach Boys in *Billboard* singles and albums chart success among American bands.

Formed of students from DePaul University and another college in 1968, the band released their first album, *The Chicago Transit Authority,* in 1969. This album featured the hits "Beginnings" and "Does Anybody Really Know What Time It Is?" Their second album, *Chicago,* featured the hits "Make Me Smile" and "25 or 6 to 4." Their first No. 1 song was in 1976 with "If You Leave Me Now," which later won Grammy Awards for Best Pop Performance by a Group and Best Arrangement Accompanying Vocalist(s) in 1977. Their 1984 album *Chicago 17* was their best-selling ever, with hits like "Stay the Night," "You're the Inspiration," and "Hard Habit to Break." They scored another No. 1 in 1988 with "Look Away" from *Chicago 19*. Today, the band is still together after 40 years. They continue to release albums and tour to sold-out crowds.

How to Play It

The song with the unusual title features a short trumpet solo at the beginning. "Does Anybody Really Know What Time It Is?" was written by the band's keyboardist/singer Robert Lamm. The song peaked at No. 7 on the U.S. charts, released as a single only when the songs "Make Me Smile" and "25 or 6 to 4" became big hits.

The trumpet solo part is basically a jazz swing. Loughnane's first four bars are great melody lines; nothing technically flashy, but just perfect phrases! In measure 6, he hangs on a high B, the 13th of the chord, tying it over into the next chord where it becomes the ninth. This adds some harmonic color to the solo. The last two bars of the solo are a part of the arrangement, played with the rest of the horns.

Be sure to swing all the eighth notes.

"It has definitely been a blur at times…"
–Lee Loughnane
on his long career

Vital Stats

Trumpet player: Lee Loughnane

Song: "Does Anybody Really Know What Time It Is?"

Album: *The Chicago Transit Authority*

Age at time of recording: 22

Trumpet: Getzen

Mouthpiece: unknown

Photo by Michael Ochs Archives/Getty Images

Chicago

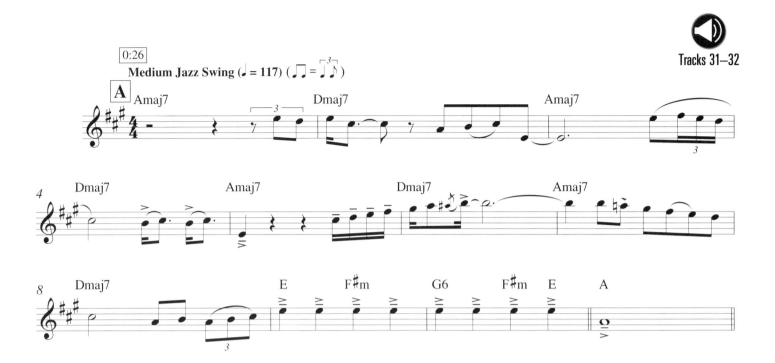

Sidney Lazar

The music for the movie *The Godfather* is as famous as the film itself. Play that haunting trumpet melody and suddenly the mood in the room will change!

Sidney "Sid" Lazar was born in 1926 in Los Angeles, California. At age eight, he started playing a cornet that was borrowed from the Los Angeles City Schools. His parents soon bought him a second-hand King trumpet, later transferring to an Olds. His first teacher was Vesey Walker. When he was 14, he became a student of Vladimir Drucker, principal trumpet for the Los Angeles Philharmonic. Together they studied symphonic repertoire. Sidney was already playing band music with solos like "Stars in a Velvety Sky," "Brides of the Waves," and "Carnival of Venice."

Lazar's professional career started when he was 16, playing fourth trumpet with the L.A. Philharmonic at the Hollywood Bowl. Before entering the army in 1944, he was just starting to get calls for recording dates. After World War II, Sidney went back to L.A. and attended the University of Southern California, graduating with a Bachelor of Music degree in 1950. As a result of his work on film scores like *High Noon*, he started establishing himself as a lead trumpet player in Hollywood. In 1956, Lazar signed a contract at Paramount Studios. As a first-call session player, he recorded for many films, including *The Tin Star, The Ten Commandments,* and famously *The Godfather* and *The Godfather, Part II*. Sidney also performed many concerts and recordings with composers Igor Stravinsky, Henry Mancini, and Elmer Bernstein.

Today, Lazar is retired and hasn't touched the trumpet in over two decades.

Courtesy of Sidney Lazar

Sidney Lazar

Composer Giovanni "Nino" Rota Rinaldi was born on December 3, 1911 in Milan, Italy. As a child prodigy, he wrote his first oratorio at age 11. He studied composition at the Santa Cecilia Academy in Rome, then moved to the U.S., where he lived from 1930 to 1932. He attended the Curtis Institute in Philadelphia on a scholarship, later returning to Italy where he received a degree in literature from the University of Milan. From 1930 to 1979, Rota composed 170 scores, many for famed filmmaker Frederico Fellini. He also wrote operas, ballets, and chamber works.

From 1950 to 1978, Rota had a teaching career as director at the Liceo Musicale in Bari, Italy. Among his composition students was the well-known classical conductor Riccardo Muti.

Rota is most famous for composing the music for *The Godfather* and *The Godfather, Part II*. For the latter, he received an Academy Award for Best Original Score in 1974.

Nino Rota died of heart failure in Rome on April 10, 1979.

How to Play It

The trumpet solo from *The Godfather* is one of the most identifiable melodies in cinematic music history. Conjuring up many emotions of darkness, due to the movie's content, its melody is haunting and somber.

The intro is scored for unaccompanied solo trumpet. Originally a Sicilian lullaby, the melody is featured throughout the movie with different orchestral configurations. (For the purposes of this book, both the solo and rhythm accompaniment are included.) Think classical trumpet playing, with a healthy dose of wide vibrato.

"I was told it was a Sicilian lullaby. I immediately thought of teddy bears et cetera and started playing warmly, as for Brahms' Lullaby. I was told 'No, no! It's a lullaby, but we want it somber, gloomy, melancholy.' Several weeks later I was called back to re-record it, playing the entire theme alone."

–Sidney Lazar

Vital Stats

Trumpet player: Sidney Lazar

Song: "The Godfather Waltz"

Album: *The Godfather: Music from the Original Motion Picture Soundtrack*

Age at time of recording: 46

Trumpet: Benge

Mouthpiece: Purviance Custom Made

Nino Rota

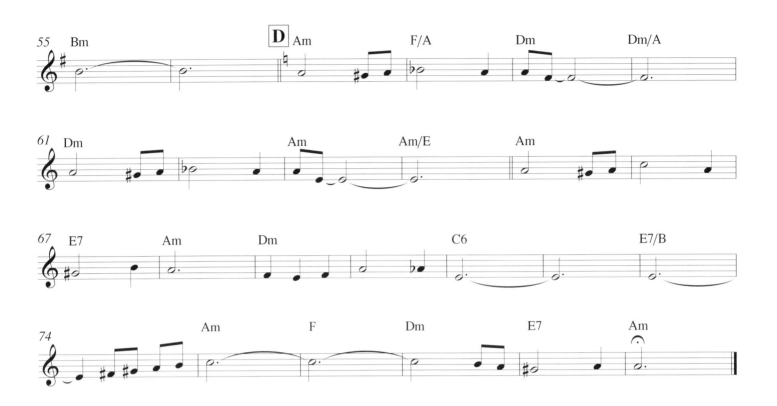

Maynard Ferguson

Maynard Ferguson's version of "MacArthur Park" made an already famous song more popular as an instrumental.

Walter Maynard Ferguson was born on May 4, 1928 in Verdun, Quebec. He was considered a child prodigy, playing piano and violin by age four. (His mother was a violinist.) He was enrolled in the French Conservatory of Music at age nine, and by the time he hit his late teens he was leading his own bands. Moving to the U.S. in 1948, he joined Stan Kenton's band in 1950, winning *Down Beat* magazine's poll

for Best Trumpet between 1950 and 1952. He also played with Charlie Barnet and Jimmy Dorsey. After leaving Kenton's band, he quickly became a first-call studio musician, playing on over 45 movie soundtracks. When his studio responsibilities prevented him from playing clubs, he decided to quit the studio scene and form his own group. In 1956, Ferguson led the famous Birdland Dream Band, featuring an all-star line up of musicians that included trombonist Jimmy Cleveland and saxophonists Al Cohn and Herb Geller. In 1959, he played the world premiere of Bill Russo's Symphony

No. 2 ("Titans") with the New York Philharmonic Orchestra, conducted by Leonard Bernstein. Only a small number

Maynard Ferguson

of players could have handled the extremely high trumpet notes practically made for Ferguson.

After a long, personal spiritual break in the mid 1960s, he signed with CBS Records in England in 1969, forming his own big band of British musicians. He recorded trumpet for the movie *The Ten Commandments* and scored a hit with the song "Gonna Fly Now" from the Oscar-winning movie *Rocky*. (His version hit the Top 30 when the movie version hit No. 1.) The album *Conquistador* went gold, while he continued to release dozens of albums throughout the '70s and '80s. Ever the workaholic, Maynard played performances and clinics all the way up to his death.

Maynard Ferguson died on August 23, 2006 in Ojai, California. He was 78 years old.

How to Play It

Written by Jimmy Webb, "MacArthur Park" was first recorded by actor/singer Richard Harris, whose version won a Grammy for Best Arrangement Accompanying Vocalist(s) in 1968. Donna Summer's 1978 disco arrangement was also a huge hit, reaching No. 1 for three weeks, and lasting even longer on *Billboard*'s Hot Dance Club Songs – for five weeks at No. 1.

Arranged by Adrian Drover, "MacArthur Park" became one of Maynard's signature big band pieces. The song was recorded on the album *M.F. Horn 4 & 5: Live at Jimmy's*. There is also a studio version on *The Essence of Maynard Ferguson*. The solo is basically the famous melody

as only Maynard can perform it. The beginning is played using a wide vibrato. Starting at measure 7, the melody is played up an octave. Between measures 12–15 the ensemble takes over, with Maynard coming back in with pickups to measure 16. The melody now is in the trumpet high range, played with a loud, bright sound. The solo ends with a high A.

"Change is always happening. That's one of the wonderful things about jazz music."

–Maynard Ferguson

Vital Stats

Trumpet player: Maynard Ferguson

Song: "MacArthur Park"

Album: *M.F. Horn 4 & 5: Live at Jimmy's*

Age at time of recording: 45

Trumpet: Holton

Mouthpiece: Jet-Tone

Photo by Michael Ochs Archives/Getty Images

Jimmy Webb

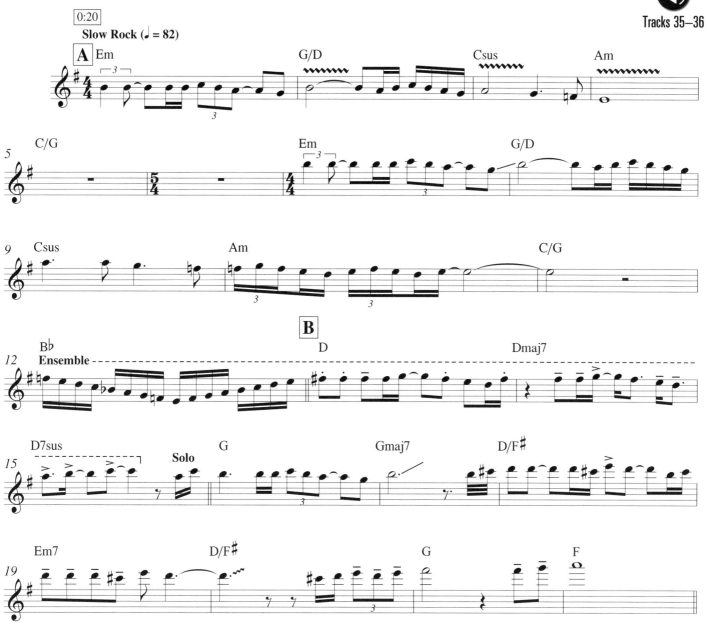

Chuck Mangione

"Feels So Good" is one of those songs that everyone has heard of and knows by heart!

Charles Frank Mangione was born on November 29, 1940 in Rochester, New York. He started playing the trumpet at age 10, listening to Stan Kenton, Count Basie, and Chet Baker while in high school. His first inspiration and idol was Dizzy Gillespie. With his brother Gap Mangione on piano, he formed the popular jazz group the Jazz Brothers in the 1950s, signing with Riverside Records. He studied at the Eastman School of Music from 1958 to 1963, earning a Bachelor of Music degree. He joined Art Blakey and the Jazz Messengers on the recommendation of Gillespie. After Blakey's band, he went on to play with Kai Winding, Maynard Ferguson, and Woody Herman. He also became director of the Eastman Jazz Ensemble from 1968 to 1972.

In 1970, Mangione recorded the live concert album *Friends and Love* with the Rochester Philharmonic Orchestra. The LP was a huge hit, and opened the door for him to sign with A&M Records. Playing flugelhorn exclusively, his song "Chase the Clouds Away," featured on his first album of the same name, was used in the 1976 Summer Olympics. He received his first Grammy Award in 1977 for "Bellavia," named for his mother, for Best Instrumental Composition. His classic, best-selling LP *Feels So Good* peaked at No. 2 on the *Billboard* album charts, thanks to the title song, eventually selling over two million copies. After *Feels So Good,* Mangione wrote the soundtrack music for the film *The*

Chuck Mangione

Children of Sanchez. That album went gold and garnered his second Grammy Award in 1979 – this time for Best Pop Instrumental Performance. His song "Give It All You Got" was used for the 1980 Winter Olympics, and the following year he composed the music for the movie *The Cannonball Run.*

Today, Mangione still tours and records, and had a recurring speaking role on the TV show *King of the Hill.*

Interesting fact: Mangione's signature hat was the recommendation of the record label after he wore it on an early album cover. According to a comment he once made in an interview, he doesn't shower with it.

"I celebrate it every day; it put my two daughters through college and introduced my music to the world."

–Chuck Mangione
on "Feels So Good"

© David Redfern / Redferns / Getty

Vital Stats

Trumpet player: Chuck Mangione

Song: "Feels So Good"

Album: *Feels So Good*

Age at time of recording: 36

Trumpet: Calicchio Flugelhorn

Mouthpiece: Giardinelli Custom

How to Play It

"Feels So Good" was written and produced by Mangione, peaking at No. 4 on the *Billboard* Hot 100. It was also nominated for a Grammy Award for Record of the Year. Recently, it was voted by smooth jazz stations across the U.S. as their No. 1 song of all time. There are two versions: the album version clocks in at nearly ten minutes, and the radio edit version is close to three-and-a-half minutes.

The solo is basically just the song's melody. Played on flugelhorn, make sure to use vibrato on all note values a half note and longer. Like the original reading, the saxophone enters the song at measure 10, playing counterpoint and harmony till the end. Make sure you play all notated articulations.

Chuck Mangione

Tracks 37–38

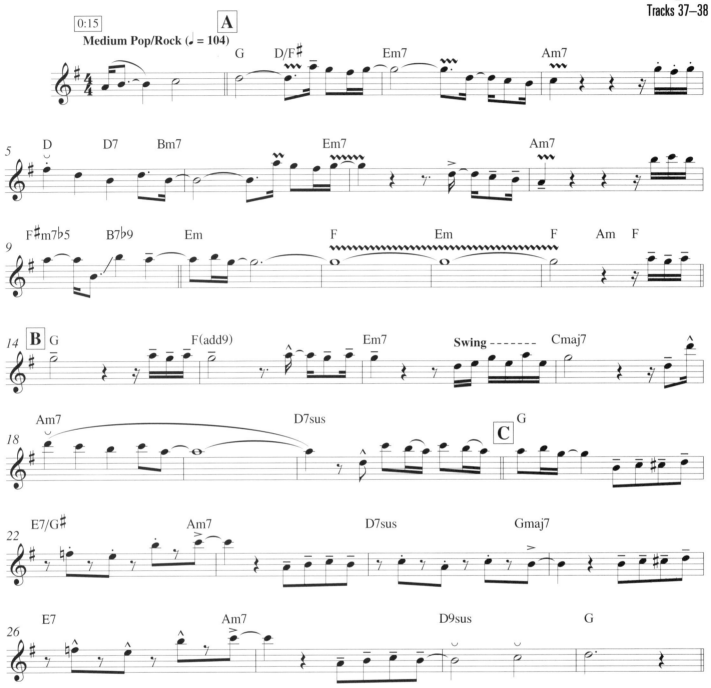

Freddie Hubbard

Who would've guessed that, hidden on the classic Billy Joel album *52nd Street*, was an amazing jazz solo by the great Freddie Hubbard?

Frederick Dewayne Hubbard was born on April 7, 1938 in Indianapolis, Indiana. He started playing the mellophone in junior high, later switching to trumpet in high school. He studied trumpet at the Arthur Jordan Conservatory of Music with Max Woodbury, principal trumpet with the Indianapolis Symphony Orchestra. He worked with guitarist Wes Montgomery in his teens, moving to New York at age 20. He immediately started playing with top jazz musicians like Slide Hampton, Sonny Rollins, and Eric Dolphy. Quincy Jones first got him into the studio scene, playing commercial jobs. In 1960, Hubbard made his first record as a leader for Blue Note, *Open Sesame*. The next year he replaced Lee Morgan in Art Blakey's Jazz Messengers, recording eight albums up until 1966. He also played on many classic jazz recordings with Wayne Shorter, Herbie Hancock, and Oliver Nelson. Some of his famous early solo albums are *Ready for Freddie, Hub-tones,* and *Breaking Point.*

In the 1970s, Hubbard achieved popular success with crossover albums like *Red Clay, Straight Life,* and *First Light,* which received a Grammy Award for Best Jazz Performance by a Group in 1972. In 1992, Hubbard ruptured his upper lip and developed an infection, which made a huge impact on his playing in his later years. In his career, he made over 300 records.

Freddie Hubbard

Hubbard died of complications from a heart attack on December 29, 2008. He was 70 years old.

William Martin "Billy" Joel was born on May 9, 1949 in the Bronx, New York. He started playing piano at an early age, loving classical music. After a brief career as a Golden Gloves boxer, he signed with Colombia Records in 1973. His first album, *Piano Man,* was a huge success. His album *The Stranger* was even bigger, with the hit song "Just the Way You Are" winning two Grammys – for Song of the Year and Record of the Year – in 1978. Joel later scored No. 1 hits with "It's Still Rock and Roll to Me," "Tell Her About It," "Uptown Girl," and 1989's "We Didn't Start the Fire." His album *Billy Joel: Greatest Hits Vol. 1 & Vol. 2* has sold over 11.5 million copies, making it the fifth best selling album in the U.S. Today, Joel continues to tour, having had recent success with the Broadway musical *Movin' Out,* which features many of his classic songs.

How to Play It

When Joel wanted a jazz sound for "Zanzibar," he called the best! The song comes from Joel's best-selling album *52nd Street,* which won Grammys for Album of the Year and Best Pop Vocal Performance. Hubbard had two different solos on the track, both equally great.

Billy Joel

SOLO 1

An up-tempo jazz swing, Hubbard does his "thing," playing amazing jazz lines. Using such diverse rhythms at such a fast tempo is simply stunning. Freddie starts the solo by quoting Gershwin's "Summertime," before playing a terrific bebop phrase in measures 6–8. In measure 6, notice the ♯5 and ♯4 that move into the chord-tone D on the downbeat of measure 7. Measure 9 starts on the ninth, moving diatonically in half-note triplets up to the ♯4 and back down. Measure 10 outlines the upper chord extensions – the ninth, 11th, and 13th – back down into measure 13. His use of half-note triplets in measure 22 again changes the pace of the solo. Measures 26 and 27 use a fast, ascending diminished scale up to the C♯ dim 7 chord. Measure 30 goes back to the original half-time feel of the song, before Hubbard plays his signature lip trill, into a descending line that seems to shift the time signature.

SOLO 2

Here's another jaw-dropping solo, played with some serious eighth-note jazz lines. Opening with a rhythm vamp for the first four bars, measure 5 then starts the up-tempo swing. Notice the use of diverse rhythms throughout the solo. Measures 36 to 41 feature another Freddie signature lick, played very fast, almost like a blur. Measure 49 is basically a fast run up to each of those written notes. The solo fades out around measure 50.

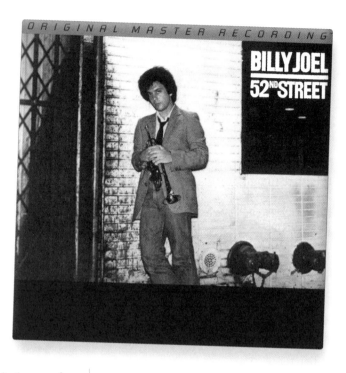

"What made my style different was a whole lot of jumps – strenuous ideas."

–Freddie Hubbard

Vital Stats

Trumpet Player: Freddie Hubbard

Song: "Zanzibar"

Album: *52nd Street*

Age at time of recording: 40

Trumpet: Calicchio

Mouthpiece: Bach 6

SOLO 1

Words and Music by Billy Joel
© 1978, 1984 IMPULSIVE MUSIC

SOLO 2

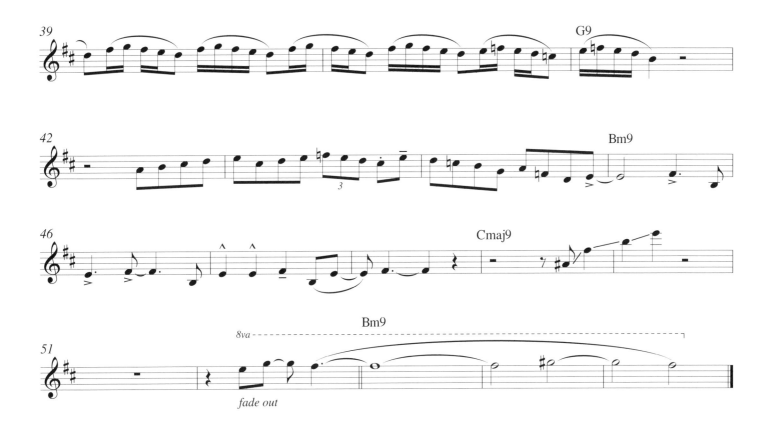

Herb Alpert

Herb Alpert may be the most successful trumpet player in music history, hands down. His instrumental hits with Herb Alpert & the Tijuana Brass and his huge success as the "A" of A&M Records confirm the fact that he has the gold (or platinum) touch.

Herbert Alpert was born on March 31, 1935 in Los Angeles, California. Growing up in a musical family, he started playing the trumpet at age eight. He enrolled at the University of Southern California, becoming a member of the Trojan Marching Band. In 1955, he was drafted into the U.S. Army, occasionally playing trumpet at military ceremonies. After the army, he struggled to make a living playing music. His early success included co-writing Top 20 hits like "Baby Talk," "Alley-Oop," and Sam Cook's "Wonderful World." On a trip to Tijuana, Mexico, during a bullfight, Alpert first heard the sound and power of a Mariachi band. The crowd's huge reaction to the music inspired him to replicate that sonority. Soon after, Herb Alpert & the Tijuana Brass were born.

In 1962, with his friend Jerry Moss, he formed A&M Records, which became the world's largest independent record label. Recording for A&M Records, while experimenting with tracks in his garage, he wrote the tune "The Lonely Bull," which became a Top 10 hit. Other hits, like "Spanish Flea" and "A Taste of Honey" soon followed. LPs like *Whipped Cream and Other Delights* and *Going Places* were million-selling albums. In 1966, the Tijuana Brass had sold over 13 million records, more than the Beatles. *The Guinness Book of World Records* acknowledged Alpert for having five albums in the Top 20 *Billboard* Pop Charts simultaneously. Another unexpected No. 1 hit came Alpert's way with his vocal recording of "The Guy's in Love with You" in 1968.

Photo by Gems / Getty

Herb Alpert & the Tijuana Brass

In 1979, to help save his financially strapped A&M Records, he recorded the song "Rise," which became a No. 1, Grammy-winning song. A&M Records was saved, later signing major acts like the Police, Janet Jackson, Styx, and Carole King. With five No. 1 hits, eight Grammy Awards, 15 gold records, 14 platinum records, and 72 million records worldwide, Alpert is by far the most commercially successful trumpet player in history.

Today, Herb Alpert is an established sculptor and painter. He donates money to many charities and organizations, mostly music-related, and occasionally performs with his wife, singer Lani Hall.

Herb Alpert

How to Play It

"Rise" was written by Randy "Badazz" Alpert and Andy Armer. It was Alpert's fifth No. 1 hit from the album of the same name, also winning a Grammy for Best Pop Instrumental. The song received an extra boost of promotion when it was featured on the ABC-TV soap opera *General Hospital,* helping it sell more than two million copies. It was later sampled on the worldwide No. 1 hit "Hypnotize" by rapper Notorious B.I.G. in 1997. Like "Feels So Good" (see page 58), the famous melody is the solo. Be sure to play it with a wide vibrato on note values a half note and longer, and play all notated articulations.

"Jerry [Moss] and I had A&M [Records] on a handshake."

–Herb Alpert

Vital Stats

Trumpet player: Herb Alpert

Song: "Rise"

Album: *Rise*

Age at time of recording: 44

Trumpet: Chicago Benge

Mouthpiece: Bach

Robert DiVall

Of the famous TV theme songs that feature trumpet, the one for *Dynasty* remains the most memorable.

Trumpeter Robert DiVall was a studio session player who graduated from UCLA in the early 1940s, serving in the Army Air Corps and various bands throughout World War II. After the war, he worked for several Los Angeles radio orchestras until Alfred Wallenstein, then music director of the L.A. Philharmonic, engaged him as a member of the orchestra's trumpet section. A year later, he was promoted to principal trumpet, holding this position until 1982. He was a member of the Hollywood Bowl Pops Orchestra and taught trumpet at UCLA for many years as a part-time member of the music faculty. His film credits include *Indiana Jones and the Last Crusade, Red Dawn, Inner Space,* as well as the TV theme *Dynasty*. DiVall was also featured on the Los Angeles Philharmonic's recording of Gustav Mahler's Symphony No. 3, conducted by Zubin Mehta.

L–R: Robert DiVall, Irving Bush, Tom Stevens, Mario Guarneri

Composer William ("Bill") Conti was born on April 13, 1942 in Providence, Rhode Island. He learned the piano from his father, an accomplished player, eventually taking bassoon lessons. He studied composition at Louisiana State University, later earning a master's degree from Juilliard. In 1967, he moved to Italy, where he first broke into film scoring. Returning to the U.S in 1976, he shot to fame with his score for the Oscar-winning film *Rocky*. The soundtrack went platinum, with the main theme, "Gonna Fly Now," becoming a No. 1 hit on the *Billboard* charts. It was also nominated for an Oscar for Best Original Song. Conti continued to have success with further *Rocky* film scores, as well as *North and South, For Your Eyes Only,* and *The Right Stuff,* winning an Oscar for the latter. Conti also wrote many TV show themes, including *The Colbys,*

Falcon Crest, and *Cagney and Lacey.* He was also musical director for the Academy Awards several times.

How to Play It

Session trumpet player Robert DiVall played piccolo trumpet on "Dynasty Theme." The series aired on ABC from January 1981 to May 1989. By the end of the 1984–85 season, it was the No. 1 show on TV. It lasted for nine seasons and 218 episodes.

The solo is essentially the song melody, played with a classical trumpet style. The B section, starting at measure 11, is the most difficult part of the song. Make sure you practice it slowly and play it in time with a metronome.

> *"Any musician who must curtail his kissing because of his trumpet playing will never do either very well."*
>
> –Robert DiVall

Vital Stats

Trumpet player: Robert DiVall

Song: "Dynasty Theme"

Album: TV theme song

Age at time of recording: unknown

Trumpet: unknown

Mouthpiece: unknown

Photo by Bobby Bank / WireImage / Getty

William ("Bill") Conti

By Bill Conti

Dizzy Gillespie

One of the greatest trumpeters and jazz pioneers in musical history, Dizzy Gillespie's genius expanded decades of songs, all the way up to 1982's "Do I Do."

(For Dizzy Gillespie's biographical information, see page 15.)

Stevland Hardaway Judkins ("Stevie Wonder") was born on May 13, 1950 in Saginaw, Michigan. Arriving six weeks prematurely, blood vessels had not yet reached the front of his eyes, causing his retinas to detach and leaving him blind. A child prodigy, he began playing piano, harmonica, drums, and bass as well as singing in the church choir. At age 11, he was signed to Motown Records with the name Little Stevie Wonder. By age 13, he had his first No. 1 hit with "Fingerprints (Pt. 2)," from his album *Recorded Live: The 12 Year Old Genius*. Throughout the 1970s Wonder reached even greater heights with classic, best-selling albums like *Talking Book, Innervisions, Fulfillingness' First Finale,* and *Songs in the Key of Life*. He scored more No. 1 hits with "You Are the Sunshine of My Life," "Superstition," "Sir Duke," and "Ebony and Ivory." Wonder received a Golden Globe Award and an Academy Award for Best Song for "I Just Called to Say I Love You," featured in the 1984 comedy *The Woman in Red*. He was inducted into the Rock and Roll Hall of Fame in 1989, and was named *Rolling Stone*'s ninth greatest singer of all time. With 25 Grammy Awards and ten No. 1 hits, Wonder's music continues to inspire musicians and artists, with his classic songs living on forever.

Roland Godefroy

Dizzy Gillespie

How to Play It

From one musical genius to another, Stevie Wonder employed Dizzy Gillespie to play on his song "Do I Do." It was released on the album *Stevie Wonder's Original Musiquarium I,* peaking at No. 13 on the *Billboard* Hot 100 Chart. If the reports are true, the song was taught to the band in sections, with no sheet music. Two versions were released: the 10+ minute version on the album, featuring Dizzy's solo, and the radio/single edit without the solo.

Set in the key of C♯ major, the song begins by outlining the melody before going into a jazz-inspired solo. All 16th notes are played with a jazz swing articulation. The rhythmic figure that begins at measure 9, beat 3 is the perfect set-up for the ensemble horn line, lasting to measure 14. The E♮ in measure 17 sets up the dominant seventh chord in the next measure, becoming the ♭7 of the F♯13 chord.

Antonio Cruz/ABr

Stevie Wonder

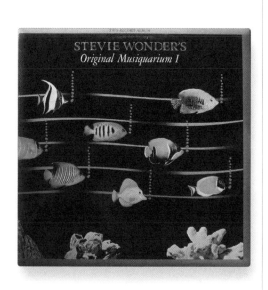

"I knew I wanted to feature Dizzy Gillespie on it, to educate people about artists in other genres of music, and to make that connection to jazz."

–Stevie Wonder on "Do I Do"

Vital Stats

Trumpet Player: Dizzy Gillespie

Song: "Do I Do"

Album: *Stevie Wonder's Original Musiquarium I*

Age at time of recording: 65

Trumpet: unknown

Mouthpiece: unknown

Tim Kellett

Simply Red's "Holding Back the Years" has become one of the timeless pop classics from the 1980s.

Tim Kellett was born on July 23, 1964 in Knaresborough, Yorkshire, England. His mother played violin, and his dad was a big classical music fan. He started playing trumpet at age seven, waiting for his front teeth to appear. Kellett studied music at the Royal Northern College of Music in Manchester, later beginning his professional career when he joined the British post-punk band the Durutti Column in 1983. Tim left the band after two years to become a founding member of the band Simply Red, where he played keyboards and

trumpet. Simply Red's 1985 debut album, *Picture Book,* sold over a million copies due to the No. 1 hit "Holding Back the Years." Kellett left Simply Red in 1995 to form the band Olive. Olive had a No. 1 UK hit in May 1997, "You're Not Alone," before going on hiatus in 2001. Tim later played with the band Nightmares on Wax.

A songwriter, keyboardist, and record producer, Kellett had success writing songs for groups like the Lighthouse Family, James Morrison, and Matthew Ward. Other collaborations include Nate James, Ella Chi, ex-Spice Girl Emma Bunton, Gareth Gates, Girls Aloud, and Taio Cruz. With Cruz, he wrote and produced the track "Never Gonna Get Us" for the 2008 *Departure* album.

Kellett currently lives and works in Derbyshire where he has a residential recording studio.

Simply Red was a British soul band that sold more than 50 million records. Formed in 1985, the band's original

Tim Kellett

name was Red. When their name was printed on posters as Simply Red, they decided to keep it. They signed with Elektra in 1985, releasing their million-selling debut album *Picture Book*. The recording featured their first hit single, "Money's Too Tight (to Mention)," and the band's biggest No. 1 hit, "Holding Back the Years." They scored another No. 1 hit in 1989 with a cover of the classic R&B tune "If You Don't Know Me by Now." The band's 1991 album *Stars* was a hit in other parts of the world, but not in the U.S. By 1994, with the growing popularity of lead singer Mick Hucknall, many of the original members departed, with Hucknall still using the name to record and tour.

In 2010, Hucknall decided to retire the band. They played their last concert at the O2 Arena in London on December 19, 2010.

How to Play It

Simply Red front man Mick Hucknall wrote "Holding Back the Years" when he was 17. This was the group's second recording of the song, reaching No. 1 on *Billboard*'s Hot 100, and hitting No. 2 on the UK Singles chart. It continues to be covered by many jazz artists and was often played on smooth jazz stations.

Oddly enough, this is a seven-bar solo. Kellett's intention was to sound reminiscent of Miles Davis, so be sure to use a Harmon mute. The solo is quite simple, but perfect, with an effective use of sustained notes and short melodic lines. Play without vibrato and observe all notated articulations.

"I used a Jo Ral Harmon Mute with the plunger removed to try and get the classic Miles Davis sound."

–Tim Kellett

Vital Stats

Trumpet Player: Tim Kellett
Song: "Holding Back the Years"
Album: *Picture Book*
Age at time of recording: 21
Trumpet: Bach Stradivarius
Mouthpiece: Bach 1/4 C

Simply Red lead singer Mike Hucknall

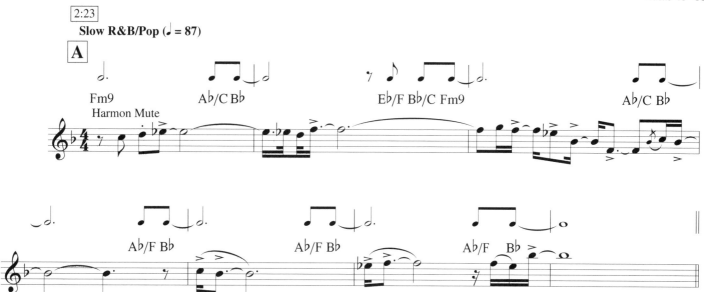

Jude Abbot

With a song title as unique as the band's name, you couldn't escape hearing the song "Tubthumping" by the band Chumbawamba in 1997.

Judith "Jude" Abbott was born on February 4, 1962 in Essex, East of England. She started playing the trumpet at age 11. Though she did not grow up in a family of musicians, she played in various youth orchestras and jazz bands throughout her adolescent years. In 1980, Jude entered Leeds University to study French and German. Finding no band to play in, she gave up the trumpet for ten years, later discovering the Peace Artistes, a Leeds-based street band.

In 1996, she joined the band Chumbawamba, singing, playing trumpet, recorder, flute, flugelhorn, and euphonium. Jude recorded ten albums with the group, including their triple-platinum *Tubthumper*. Aside from playing and touring with Chumbawamba, she played in a big band and symphony orchestra, and currently designs websites and manages a co-operative record label.

Formed in Leeds, England in 1982, Chumbawamba has spanned over three decades. Known for their anarchist politics, they were on the forefront of 1980s anarcho-punk movement. According to Jude Abbott, "Chumbawamba didn't conform very closely to most people's definition of what the band is. We were a cottage industry, and if our end product was an album or a tour, then we'd be involved in as many stages as possible along the way to its creation. Some of that was musical – writing, recording and rehearsing – but as much if not more wasn't."

The band released seven albums on indie labels, including their own Agit-

Jude Abbott

Prop label. In 1997, the band signed with EMI, causing a lot of anger with their anti-establishment fans. Their album *Tubthumper* was soon released, eventually selling over three million copies. The song "Tubthumping" peaked at No. 6 in the U.S., hitting No. 2 on the UK Singles chart. The band spent the next 18 months on a mad adventure of international touring, promo, and TV shows. (They even went onstage after Aerosmith at Madison Square Garden.) The songs "Amnesia" and "Top of the World (Ole, Ole, Ole)" were minor hits as well.

In 2012, it was announced that Chumbawamba had decided to disband.

How to Play It

The solo is pretty simple, but perfect. Measures 5–8 have harmony parts that add a nice contrast. (On Track 52, the top lead line is omitted). Play the song straight, with no vibrato.

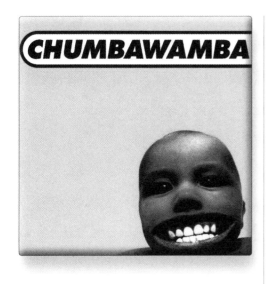

"I do remember Boff Whalley (Chumbawamba lead guitarist) suggesting the octave leap at the end of the fourth bar, which is genius, but something I dreaded doing live."

–Jude Abbot

Vital Stats

Trumpet player: Jude Abbott

Song: "Tubthumping"

Album: *Tubthumper*

Age at time of recording: 35

Trumpet: Yamaha YTR 6310Z

Mouthpiece: Vincent Bach 7C

Chumbawamba *a capella* (L-R) Neil Ferguson, Lou Watts, Boff Whalley, Jude Abbott, Phil Moody

Chris Botti

From his high profile work with Paul Simon and Sting to selling over three million albums as a solo artist, Chris Botti is becoming this generation's voice of the trumpet.

Christopher Stephen Botti was born on October 12, 1962 in Portland, Oregon. Exposed to music early by his mother, a classically trained pianist, he started playing the trumpet at age nine. Seeing Doc Severinsen play the trumpet on TV and thinking he was "cool" lit a spark in him. But it was Miles Davis's *My Funny Valentine* album that became Chris's real inspiration.

Botti attended Indiana University, studying with David Baker and Bill Adam. He also took lessons with jazz greats Woody Shaw and George Coleman. After performance stints with Buddy Rich and Frank Sinatra, he decided to try his luck in New York, becoming a first-call session player and recording music for *Nightline, Monday Night Football,* and ESPN. In the early 1990s, he toured with Paul Simon for a couple of years. Chris also produced the Grammy Award-winning *Out of the Loop* album for the Brecker Brothers in 1994. The next year, he released his premier solo album, *First Wish,* on the Verve label, later releasing two more albums for the label.

Playing as a featured soloist with Sting for his 2001 Brand New Day Tour quickly brought Chris international recognition. After the gig with Sting, Botti was bandleader for *The Caroline Rhea Show*

© Igor Vidyashev / Alamy

Chris Botti

in 2002. He was voted one of the 50 beautiful people by *People* magazine in 2004. Signed with Colombia Records, he released hit albums like *When I Fall in Love, To Love Again: The Duets,* and *Chris Botti in Boston,* which was nominated for a Grammy. The album *Italia* was nominated as well, for Best Pop Instrumental Album.

Today, Botti continues to perform to capacity crowds and to make records. Most recently, *Impressions,* his tenth studio album, peaked at No. 1 on the *Billboard* Jazz Charts.

Renee Olstead was born on June 18, 1989 in Kingwood, Texas. She began her career as a child actress, doing commercials and films. She starred on the TV show *Still Standing* from 2002 to 2006. Her first solo albums were in country genre

and did not have wide distribution. Her self-titled 2004 album (co-produced by David Foster) is considered her real debut. It was comprised of pop and jazz standards. Renee released *Skylark* in 2009 and continues to perform concerts and to pursue her acting career in movies and on TV.

How to Play It

"A Sunday Kind of Love" was first published in 1946. Though covered by many artists like Etta James and Ella Fitzgerald, Renee Olstead's version with Botti's brief eight-bar solo – recorded on Renee's self-titled debut release – speaks volumes.

Displaying a textbook solo on a vocal track, Chris uses a Harmon mute throughout. Measure 3 has the famous "Cry Me a River" quote/lick over the B♭7, altering the chord, which Botti plays fast. At this ballad tempo, it looks and sounds like "sheets of sound" à la John Coltrane, as Botti skates over the changes. Measures 7–8 were played in unison with Renee, which added an interesting effect on the original recording. Make sure to "lay back" throughout the solo, and play it in a jazz style.

"Part of me is thinking about not letting the trumpet get the best of me, which is tough."

–Chris Botti

Vital Stats

Trumpet player: Chris Botti

Song: "A Sunday Kind of Love"

Album: *Renee Olstead*

Age at time of recording: 42

Trumpet: Vintage 1939 Martin Large-Bore "Hand Craft" Committee

Mouthpiece: 1926 #3 Silver-Plated Bach, with back bore drilled out to a 13

Photo by Ryan Sanjaya

Renee Olstead

Tracks 53–54

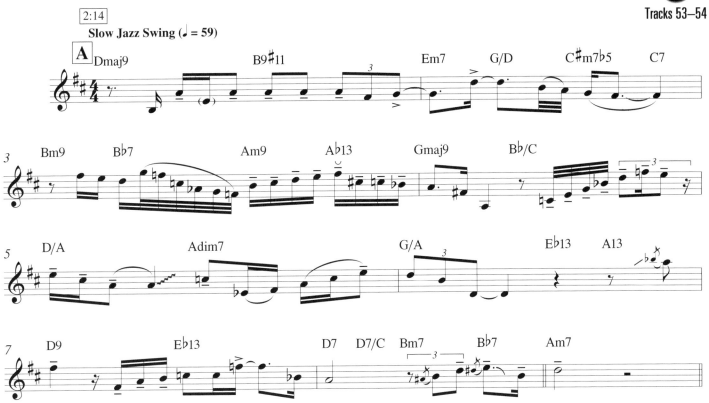

Words and Music by Louis Prima, Anita Nye Leonard, Stanley Rhodes and Barbara Belle

About the Author

Eric J. Morones hails from Racine, WI. He attended the University of Wisconsin-Whitewater, where he received a degree in communications, with a minor in music. He later did graduate work in jazz studies at the University of North Texas. Now living in Los Angeles, Eric has played, toured and/or recorded with Kelly Clarkson, the Brian Setzer Orchestra, Big Bad Voodoo Daddy, Bobby Caldwell, Steve Tyrell, Maureen McGovern, Jack Sheldon, Bill Holman, Will Kennedy, and Chad Wackerman. His sax playing is featured on the *Big Fish Audio Sample DVD Suite Grooves 1 and 2*. He has performed at the Montreux and North Sea Jazz Festivals, as well as on *The Tonight Show with Jay Leno, Dancing with the Stars, Late Night with Conan O'Brien, The Today Show, Live with Regis and Kelly,* and *Woodstock '99*.

A busy author, Eric has written the books *101 Saxophone Tips, Paul Desmond Saxophone Signature Licks,* and *25 Great Saxophone Solos* (Hal Leonard Publishing). He wrote a bi-monthly column for the *Saxophone Journal* called "From the Front Lines," and produced two Masterclass CDs for the magazine: *How to Play Pop, R&B and Smooth Jazz* and *How to Play the Blues*. Eric's first solo jazz CD, *About Time!,* is available on Arabesque Records.

ericmorones.com

About the Performer

Steve Reid has been playing professionally for over 20 years, in many bands and orchestras of varying musical styles. He received his musical training at the University of North Florida and the University of Miami. From 1990–1994, he played lead trumpet for Disneyland and Walt Disney World, and between 1994–2002 played the "Cat Anderson" book and lead trumpet with the Duke Ellington Orchestra, under the direction of Mercer Ellington. Steve also played in the pit orchestras for the Broadway productions of *Cats* and *Miss Saigon*.

In the spring of 1997, Steve played lead trumpet for Maynard Ferguson and his Big Bop Nouveau band. In 2002, he joined KC and the Sunshine Band, playing lead and solo trumpet with the band for three years. Steve also is a member of the Brian Setzer Orchestra, recording on the albums *Lonely Avenue, Wolfgang's Night Out,* and *Don't Mess with the Big Band*. With the BSO, he has performed on *Late Night with Conan O'Brien, The Tonight Show with Jay Leno, The Today Show,* and *The Rachel Ray Show*.

As a freelance musician in L.A., Steve works regularly with various artists and acts, including Prince, Al McKay and the Earth, Wind & Fire Experience. He also maintains an active guest artist and clinician schedule.

stevereidmusic.com

A R T I S T TRANSCRIPTIONS®

Artist Transcriptions are authentic, note-for-note transcriptions of today's hottest artists in jazz, pop and rock. These outstanding, accurate arrangements are in an easy-to-read format which includes all essential lines. Artist Transcriptions can be used to perform, sequence or for reference.

CLARINET
00672423	Buddy De Franco Collection	$19.95

FLUTE
00672379	Eric Dolphy Collection	$19.95
00672582	The Very Best of James Galway	$16.99
00672372	James Moody Collection – Sax and Flute	$19.95

GUITAR & BASS
00660113	The Guitar Style of George Benson	$14.95
00699072	Guitar Book of Pierre Bensusan	$29.95
00672331	Ron Carter – Acoustic Bass	$16.95
00672573	Ray Brown	$19.99
00672307	Stanley Clarke Collection	$19.95
00660115	Al Di Meola – Friday Night in San Francisco	$14.95
00604043	Al Di Meola – Music, Words, Pictures	$14.95
00672574	Al Di Meola – Pursuit of Radical Rhapsody	$22.99
00125617	Best of Herb Ellis	$19.99
00673245	Jazz Style of Tal Farlow	$19.95
00699306	Jim Hall – Exploring Jazz Guitar	$19.95
00604049	Allan Holdsworth – Reaching for the Uncommon Chord	$14.95
00699215	Leo Kottke – Eight Songs	$14.95
00672353	Joe Pass Collection	$18.95
00673216	John Patitucci	$17.99
00027083	Django Reinhardt Antholog	$14.95
00672374	Johnny Smith Guitar Solos	$19.99

PIANO & KEYBOARD
00672338	Monty Alexander Collection	$19.95
00672487	Monty Alexander Plays Standards	$19.95
00672520	Count Basie Collection	$19.95
00113680	Blues Piano Legends	$19.99
00672439	Cyrus Chestnut Collection	$19.95
00672300	Chick Corea – Paint the World	$12.95
14037739	Storyville Presents Duke Ellington	$19.99
00146105	Bill Evans – Alone	$16.99
00672537	Bill Evans at Town Hall	$16.95
00672548	The Mastery of Bill Evans	$12.95
00672425	Bill Evans – Piano Interpretations	$19.95
00672365	Bill Evans – Piano Standards	$19.95
00121885	Bill Evans – Time Remembered	$19.99
00672510	Bill Evans Trio – Vol. 1: 1959-1961	$24.95
00672511	Bill Evans Trio – Vol. 2: 1962-1965	$24.99
00672512	Bill Evans Trio – Vol. 3: 1968-1974	$24.95
00672513	Bill Evans Trio – Vol. 4: 1979-1980	$24.95
00672381	Tommy Flanagan Collection	$24.99
00672492	Benny Goodman Collection	$16.95
00672486	Vince Guaraldi Collection	$19.95
00672419	Herbie Hancock Collection	$19.95
00672438	Hampton Hawes	$19.95
14037738	Storyville Presents Earl Hines	$19.99
00672322	Ahmad Jamal Collection	$22.95
00124367	Jazz Piano Masters Play Rodgers & Hammerstein	$19.99
00672564	Best of Jeff Lorber	$17.99

00672476	Brad Mehldau Collection	$19.99
00672388	Best of Thelonious Monk	$19.99
00672389	Thelonious Monk Collection	$19.95
00672390	Thelonious Monk Plays Jazz Standards – Volume 1	$19.95
00672391	Thelonious Monk Plays Jazz Standards – Volume 2	$19.95
00672433	Jelly Roll Morton – The Piano Rolls	$12.95
00672553	Charlie Parker for Piano	$19.95
00672542	Oscar Peterson – Jazz Piano Solos	$16.95
00672562	Oscar Peterson – A Jazz Portrait of Frank Sinatra	$19.95
00672544	Oscar Peterson – Originals	$10.99
00672532	Oscar Peterson – Plays Broadway	$19.95
00672531	Oscar Peterson – Plays Duke Ellington	$19.95
00672563	Oscar Peterson – A Royal Wedding Suite	$19.99
00672569	Oscar Peterson – Tracks	$19.99
00672533	Oscar Peterson – Trios	$24.95
00672543	Oscar Peterson Trio – Canadiana Suite	$12.99
00672534	Very Best of Oscar Peterson	$22.95
00672371	Bud Powell Classics	$19.95
00672376	Bud Powell Collection	$19.95
00672507	Gonzalo Rubalcaba Collection	$19.95
00672303	Horace Silver Collection	$19.95
00672316	Art Tatum Collection	$22.95
00672355	Art Tatum Solo Book	$19.95
00673215	McCoy Tyner	$17.99
00672321	Cedar Walton Collection	$19.95
00672519	Kenny Werner Collection	$19.95
00672434	Teddy Wilson Collection	$19.95

SAXOPHONE
00672566	The Mindi Abair Collection	$14.99
00673244	Julian "Cannonball" Adderley Collection	$19.95
00673237	Michael Brecker	$19.95
00672429	Michael Brecker Collection	$19.95
00672315	Benny Carter Plays Standards	$22.95
00672394	James Carter Collection	$19.95
00672349	John Coltrane Plays Giant Steps	$19.95
00672529	John Coltrane – Giant Steps	$14.99
00672494	John Coltrane – A Love Supreme	$14.95
00307393	John Coltrane – Omnibook: C Instruments	$24.99
00307391	John Coltrane – Omnibook: B-flat Instruments	$24.99
00307392	John Coltrane – Omnibook: E-flat Instruments	$24.99
00307394	John Coltrane – Omnibook: Bass Clef Instruments	$24.99
00672493	John Coltrane Plays "Coltrane Changes"	$19.95
00672453	John Coltrane Plays Standards	$19.95
00673233	John Coltrane Solos	$22.95
00672328	Paul Desmond Collection	$19.95
00672379	Eric Dolphy Collection	$19.95

00672530	Kenny Garrett Collection	$19.95
00699375	Stan Getz	$19.95
00672377	Stan Getz – Bossa Novas	$19.95
00672375	Stan Getz – Standards	$18.95
00673254	Great Tenor Sax Solos	$18.99
00672523	Coleman Hawkins Collection	$19.95
00673252	Joe Henderson – Selections from "Lush Life" & "So Near So Far"	$19.95
00672330	Best of Joe Henderson	$22.95
00672350	Tenor Saxophone Standards	$18.95
00673239	Best of Kenny G	$19.95
00673229	Kenny G – Breathless	$19.95
00672462	Kenny G – Classics in the Key of G	$19.95
00672485	Kenny G – Faith: A Holiday Album	$14.95
00672373	Kenny G – The Moment	$19.95
00672498	Jackie McLean Collection	$19.95
00672372	James Moody Collection – Sax and Flute	$19.95
00672416	Frank Morgan Collection	$19.95
00672539	Gerry Mulligan Collection	$19.95
00672352	Charlie Parker Collection	$19.95
00672561	Best of Sonny Rollins	$19.95
00102751	Sonny Rollins with the Modern Jazz Quartet	$17.99
00675000	David Sanborn Collection	$17.95
00672491	New Best of Wayne Shorter	$19.95
00672550	The Sonny Stitt Collection	$19.95
00672350	Tenor Saxophone Standards	$18.95
00672567	The Best of Kim Waters	$17.99
00672524	Lester Young Collection	$19.95

TROMBONE
00672332	J.J. Johnson Collection	$19.95
00672489	Steve Turré Collection	$19.99

TRUMPET
00672557	Herb Alpert Collection	$16.99
00672480	Louis Armstrong Collection	$17.95
00672481	Louis Armstrong Plays Standards	$17.95
00672435	Chet Baker Collection	$19.95
00672556	Best of Chris Botti	$19.95
00672448	Miles Davis – Originals, Vol. 1	$19.95
00672451	Miles Davis – Originals, Vol. 2	$19.95
00672450	Miles Davis – Standards, Vol. 1	$19.95
00672449	Miles Davis – Standards, Vol. 2	$19.95
00672479	Dizzy Gillespie Collection	$19.95
00673214	Freddie Hubbard	$14.95
00672382	Tom Harrell – Jazz Trumpet	$19.95
00672363	Jazz Trumpet Solos	$9.95
00672506	Chuck Mangione Collection	$19.95
00672525	Arturo Sandoval – Trumpet Evolution	$19.95

HAL•LEONARD®
7777 W. BLUEMOUND RD. P.O. BOX 13819 MILWAUKEE, WI 53213

Visit our web site for a complete listing of our titles with songlists at
www.halleonard.com

1116

Prices and availability subject to change without notice.

HAL•LEONARD INSTRUMENTAL PLAY-ALONG

Your favorite songs are arranged just for solo instrumentalists with this outstanding series. Each book includes a great full-accompaniment play-along audio so you can sound just like a pro! Check out www.halleonard.com to see all the titles available.

Chart Hits

All About That Bass • All of Me • Happy • Radioactive • Roar • Say Something • Shake It Off • A Sky Full of Stars • Someone like You • Stay with Me • Thinking Out Loud • Uptown Funk.

_____	00146207	Flute	$12.99
_____	00146208	Clarinet	$12.99
_____	00146209	Alto Sax	$12.99
_____	00146210	Tenor Sax	$12.99
_____	00146211	Trumpet	$12.99
_____	00146212	Horn	$12.99
_____	00146213	Trombone	$12.99
_____	00146214	Violin	$12.99
_____	00146215	Viola	$12.99
_____	00146216	Cello	$12.99

Coldplay

Clocks • Every Teardrop Is a Waterfall • Fix You • In My Place • Lost! • Paradise • The Scientist • Speed of Sound • Trouble • Violet Hill • Viva La Vida • Yellow.

_____	00103337	Flute	$12.99
_____	00103338	Clarinet	$12.99
_____	00103339	Alto Sax	$12.99
_____	00103340	Tenor Sax	$12.99
_____	00103341	Trumpet	$12.99
_____	00103342	Horn	$12.99
_____	00103343	Trombone	$12.99
_____	00103344	Violin	$12.99
_____	00103345	Viola	$12.99
_____	00103346	Cello	$12.99

Disney Greats

Arabian Nights • Hawaiian Roller Coaster Ride • It's a Small World • Look Through My Eyes • Yo Ho (A Pirate's Life for Me) • and more.

_____	00841934	Flute	$12.99
_____	00841935	Clarinet	$12.99
_____	00841936	Alto Sax	$12.99
_____	00841937	Tenor Sax	$12.95
_____	00841938	Trumpet	$12.99
_____	00841939	Horn	$12.95
_____	00841940	Trombone	$12.95
_____	00841941	Violin	$12.99
_____	00841942	Viola	$12.95
_____	00841943	Cello	$12.99
_____	00842078	Oboe	$12.99

Great Themes

Bella's Lullaby • Chariots of Fire • Get Smart • Hawaii Five-O Theme • I Love Lucy • The Odd Couple • Spanish Flea • and more.

_____	00842468	Flute	$12.99
_____	00842469	Clarinet	$12.99
_____	00842470	Alto Sax	$12.99
_____	00842471	Tenor Sax	$12.99
_____	00842472	Trumpet	$12.99
_____	00842473	Horn	$12.99
_____	00842474	Trombone	$12.99
_____	00842475	Violin	$12.99
_____	00842476	Viola	$12.99
_____	00842477	Cello	$12.99

Lennon & McCartney Favorites

All You Need Is Love • A Hard Day's Night • Here, There and Everywhere • Hey Jude • Let It Be • Nowhere Man • Penny Lane • She Loves You • When I'm Sixty-Four • and more.

_____	00842600	Flute	$12.99
_____	00842601	Clarinet	$12.99
_____	00842603	Tenor Sax	$12.99
_____	00842604	Trumpet	$12.99
_____	00842605	Horn	$12.99
_____	00842607	Violin	$12.99
_____	00842608	Viola	$12.99
_____	00842609	Cello	$12.99

Popular Hits

Breakeven • Fireflies • Halo • Hey, Soul Sister • I Gotta Feeling • I'm Yours • Need You Now • Poker Face • Viva La Vida • You Belong with Me • and more.

_____	00842511	Flute	$12.99
_____	00842512	Clarinet	$12.99
_____	00842513	Alto Sax	$12.99
_____	00842514	Tenor Sax	$12.99
_____	00842515	Trumpet	$12.99
_____	00842516	Horn	$12.99
_____	00842517	Trombone	$12.99
_____	00842518	Violin	$12.99
_____	00842519	Viola	$12.99
_____	00842520	Cello	$12.99

Songs from Frozen, Tangled and Enchanted

Do You Want to Build a Snowman? • For the First Time in Forever • Happy Working Song • I See the Light • In Summer • Let It Go • Mother Knows Best • That's How You Know • True Love's First Kiss • When Will My Life Begin • and more.

_____	00126921	Flute	$12.99
_____	00126922	Clarinet	$12.99
_____	00126923	Alto Sax	$12.99
_____	00126924	Tenor Sax	$12.99
_____	00126925	Trumpet	$12.99
_____	00126926	Horn	$12.99
_____	00126927	Trombone	$12.99
_____	00126928	Violin	$12.99
_____	00126929	Viola	$12.99
_____	00126930	Cello	$12.99

Top Hits

Adventure of a Lifetime • Budapest • Die a Happy Man • Ex's & Oh's • Fight Song • Hello • Let It Go • Love Yourself • One Call Away • Pillowtalk • Stitches • Writing's on the Wall.

_____	00171073	Flute	$12.99
_____	00171074	Clarinet	$12.99
_____	00171075	Alto Sax	$12.99
_____	00171106	Tenor Sax	$12.99
_____	00171107	Trumpet	$12.99
_____	00171108	Horn	$12.99
_____	00171109	Trombone	$12.99
_____	00171110	Violin	$12.99
_____	00171111	Viola	$12.99
_____	00171112	Cello	$12.99

Wicked

As Long As You're Mine • Dancing Through Life • Defying Gravity • For Good • I'm Not That Girl • Popular • The Wizard and I • and more.

_____	00842236	Flute	$12.99
_____	00842237	Clarinet	$11.99
_____	00842238	Alto Saxophone	$11.95
_____	00842239	Tenor Saxophone	$11.95
_____	00842240	Trumpet	$11.99
_____	00842241	Horn	$11.95
_____	00842242	Trombone	$11.95
_____	00842243	Violin	$11.99
_____	00842244	Viola	$12.99
_____	00842245	Cello	$12.99

Prices, contents, and availability subject to change without notice.
Disney characters and artwork © Disney Enterprises, Inc.

HAL•LEONARD®